By Dan Quinn '81

To C-Company
Thanks & Gig 'Em!
Dan Quinn '81

The author recognizes "Aggies" and other service marks of Texas A&M
University and appreciates Texas A&M for its use of these in this book.

To mom and dad, for without you these experiences would have never been possible. To mamaw, for the inspiration and drive you have given me. And to my wife, Cindy, for your constant love and support and for allowing me to reminisce. This book is dedicated to all Aggies — past, present and future.

TABLE OF CONTENTS

1. What Am I Doing Here? 1

2. Why Me?...9

3. In Trouble Already 14

4. Pisshead Initiation 26

5. My First Crap Out 34

6. Late Night Excitement 47

7. A Freshman's Privilege 54

8. Guide-On Bearer 59

9. What Does Your Mother Call You?.......................................70

10. The Last Crap Out 77

11. Final Review 82

12. Pissheads!...86

13. Surgebutts! 93

14. From Frog to Zip..101

15. Midnight Yell Practice 110

16. March In! 115

17. Austin, Here We Come! 122

18. Former Students 129

Glossary 134

Where They Are Now 137

CHAPTER 1

WHAT AM I DOING HERE?

Thirty push-ups?" Martin hollered! "Is that all you can do, dad? Even I can do more than that!"

My five year old son was probably right. I hadn't kept up the routine like I should have.

"Look," I replied, "if your little brother, Ryan, wasn't sitting on my back, I could whip off a class set in no time!"

"What's a class set?" he asked with a look of confusion on his face.

My mind instantly flashed back to my freshman year at Texas A&M University ...

"Push 'till I get tired!" Mr. Tevis suddenly screamed while I, along with the rest of the fish in Gator Two, instinctively dropped and began pushing.

"One, sir! Two, sir! Three, sir!" we counted.

"Stop and start over!" Mr. Brown interrupted. "You guys can't even count together! How do you expect to work as a team? Don't you guys have any pride?"

"Yes, sir!" we chorused in unison, our voices echoing throughout the old brick Corps dorm. I realized it was just my imagination when my three year old, Ryan, pounced on me, jolting me back to the present.

I recalled when, as freshmen in the Corps of Cadets at Texas A&M, we were often told to drop and give the upperclassmen a "class set" of push-ups. A class set of push-ups equalled eighty-one, since we would one day be the class of 1981. We actually got to the point where it was no big deal, whispering sarcastic comments about the "pissheads," a nickname for sophomores in the Corps, while still in the push-up position.

"Tell me about the fish," Martin said, as I attempted to catch my breath.

"Well," I began, "it was a freshman's privilege to get away with anything that he could, as long as he didn't get caught."

"Did you ever get caught?" he asked.

"A couple of times," I chuckled, as my wife's eyes rolled, knowing what was about to happen.

I vividly remembered the overwhelming feeling of helplessness I experienced as my father and brother drove me around the huge campus of Texas A&M for the first time. The long 12-hour drive from Arkansas made me a bit apprehensive, but my anticipation of the freedom college life offered, coupled with eighteen years of parental dependance, left me feeling a bit sick to my stomach. I knew this was what I had wanted, but being dropped off thirteen hundred miles from familiar surroundings on a Central Texas prairie with a campus the size of a small city made wonder what kind of decision I had recently made.

All I knew about Texas A&M was that it happened to be located somewhere in Texas and my high school sweetheart, Kathy, had also made plans to attend in two years. Her father, a colonel in the Air Force, had attended years earlier when it was an all-male military institution. The Corps of Cadets now was an optional part of the curriculum and the university had become coed several years earlier. Other than that, I was completely in the dark.

I had decided to enroll at the last minute, was surprisingly accepted, then managed to finagle my way into Fish Camp. The camp was designed to orient freshmen to college life. Kathy's oldest sister was attending A&M and had been selected to be a Fish Camp counselor. Her description of the camp convinced me to attend. I figured it would be a good way to meet a few people prior to the first semester.

After the long drive, my father and older brother, Bill, dropped me off in front of the Memorial Student Center on campus, amidst a sea of unfamiliar faces.

"Good luck," my father said as the van drove off back to Arkansas.

"See 'ya at Christmas!" Bill hollered with a smile as they drove away.

I suddenly experienced that vacuous loneliness which a traveler encounters in a strange, unknown city, yet looked forward to the new life I had only recently chosen. I had always been somewhat gregarious, but this seemed a little ridiculous. I came very close to catching the next bus back home to Arkansas and convincing my parents to allow me to enroll in the local community college. After all, I had only decided to go to college recently, and it was a free country; I did have the right to change my mind. But, the first semester's tuition had already been paid, and I doubt my parents would have bought any story I could have conjured up.

We were quickly ushered, by name, into several groups and told to congregate at a large outdoor fountain next to a huge building called Rudder Tower. After a quick orientation by several enthusiastic counselors, we were loaded onto busses and hauled approximately three hours away to a secluded campsite. During the bus ride, we were introduced to several unique Aggie traditions, the first of which was yelling. As our counselor gave specific hand and body signals, we were taught to yell specific words that corresponded with each of his unique gyrations. I soon realized that this would be the first of many traditions I would be introduced to during the bus ride.

We were told about events like midnight yell practice, a peculiar demonstration of school spirit that takes place in the football stadium at midnight prior to each home football game. We were told that thousands of students, parents, and even grandparents, who were still full of something called the "Aggie spirit," attended these midnight yell practices in hopes of cheering the Aggie football team on to victory the following day.

"Sure," I thought to myself. "I'll believe it when I see it." Another tradition taught during the ride was called "Elephant Walk."

"Ask a fish in the Corps of Cadets to tell you about Elephant Walk," the counselor began, "and he'll say something like 'Sir, before the Thanksgiving day football game each year, the seniors gather at the flag pole on military walk and wander aimlessly about the campus like old elephants about to die. This symbolizes the fact that they will graduate the following spring and will be of no further use to the twelfth man, sir!' Actually," he continued, "it's the juniors' opportunity to make fun of the seniors, then get in trouble for it."

"What in the world is a fish?" I wondered silently. "And, what does all of this have to do with me? I'm just here to get an education, not to catch some sort of contagious spirit." Then, just as I was becoming acquainted with a cute girl sitting next to me, he interrupted again.

"That brings me to another tradition, the Twelfth Man. You see, back in 1922 the Aggies were playing in the Dixie Classic, which is now the Cotton Bowl, against a school by the name of Center College. The Aggie football team was being overrun with injuries. Coach Dana Bible called a young man by the name of E. King Gill out of the stands to suit-up as a substitute. The student agreed to the proposition and did so. Though he never actually entered the game, his willingness to play, if needed, has inspired all Aggie students to stand throughout each football game. It shows their willingness to suit-up if called upon."

"Why would anyone want to stand up for an entire football game?" I thought to myself. "This is getting a little strange. Maybe I'd better reconsider junior college back in Arkansas."

He then went on to tell us that being an Aggie was much more than just being a student. We were to become like family to one another. One of the ways we would come to feel this way was by attending an honored tradition called "Aggie Muster." Muster, he said, was a final roll call performed annually for those Aggies who had passed away during the year. A close friend of the deceased would then answer "here" in proxy for the fallen Aggie, symbolizing their presence and the last opportunity to be accounted for.

"Muster," he said, "reminds each of us that mortality is temporary, but the bonds of friendship and camaraderie should, and will, extend beyond the grave."

The last tradition he told us about was "Bonfire." Again, the freshmen in the Corps of Cadets had their own way of explaining it. "Sir," he began as his body instinctively stiffened, "before the Thanksgiving day football game with t.u. each year, Aggies build a huge bonfire which symbolizes their burning desire to beat the hell out of t.u. and the undying spirit that all Aggies have for Texas A&M. The bonfire is set ablaze the night before the game is played in Kyle Field and Thursday before the game is played in Austin, sir!"

I later learned that t.u. was a nickname Aggies used for the University of Texas, A&M's century-old rival. They were also known as "tea sips."

"This guy must be in the Corps," someone behind me said sarcastically."

What's the Corps?" I asked, as I turned to see who had made the comment.

"Oh, it's a group of military cadets that live on campus," a large freshman behind me answered. "They're all a bit strange from what I've heard." At this point I tended to agreed with him.

We were instructed that the Bonfire, built entirely from tree trunks, gave all Aggies an opportunity to work together toward a common goal. The school had established a world record for the largest bonfire back in 1967, when the bonfire stood at 105 feet high. Because of the time involved, the height and size had since been limited by the university. He explained that prior to lighting the bonfire, an outhouse was placed on top to represent t.u.

"Should the outhouse remain intact past midnight, tradition has it the Aggies will be victorious the following day." he said. "But, should the stack of lumber fall prior to midnight, the Aggies are sure to be out-scored. By the way, Aggies never lose. We might get out-scored every now and then, but we never lose."

I viewed Fish Camp as an opportunity for me to start my new life away from the security of home and high school friends. We were encouraged to forget about all of our wonderful high school accomplishments, because now we were starting over as Aggies, each equal to the other. We were taught to be united and to be friendly. Above all, we were to be honest with others. There was no need for false pretense here. We could trust each other. "Aggies do not lie, cheat, or steal — nor do they tolerate those who do," he concluded as we arrived at camp.

"Maybe so," I thought, but I had worked hard for my high school letter jacket, and I wasn't about to give up all of my high school accomplishments just yet.

After a couple of days, these traditions began to make more sense, as we learned more about the history of this century-old land grant college. One particularly memorable experience took place in a dark room where we were encouraged to sit without talking or touching anyone around us. As soothing music played, a camp counselor took us on an imaginary journey. We boarded a fictitious airplane and were encouraged to leave all of the things we didn't like about ourselves behind. This was our opportunity to change and begin anew amongst strangers. I could hear people around me begin to cry and, as the lights were turned on, the moisture in the eyes around me convinced me of its value.

On the final evening, several students, both male and female, fresh-men and counselors, cried openly as they expressed their appreciation for the friendships made during the three-day outing. Many egos were left behind as we finished and headed back to College Station to begin our new lives as Aggies. I felt as if I were no longer returning to a huge, intimidating university. I had some friends now. It felt, somehow, as if I would indeed be among family.

My first semester was spent with three other guys in the Douxe Chene Apartments, an apartment complex located a few miles south of the campus. A high school friend, by the name of Dave Darling, allowed me to room with him and two former roommates. Dave and I had become acquainted through our high school basketball team in Arkansas where our fathers were assigned to the same Air Force base.

Once settled, I began the task of familiarizing myself with the huge campus. I determined my class route days in advance of the first class day, in order to eliminate the possibility of my worst nightmare becoming reality. I had a continual nightmare of getting lost on campus the first week and walking into my various classes late, or missing them completely. The thought terrified me, and I was determined that it would never occur.

My first semester was an exciting one. Football games, parties, and new acquaintances left little time for idleness. I thrived on my new-found freedom, and somehow managed to pass my initial classes with unexpected ease. I made the adjustment to college life fairly easily and often found it hard to believe that I could actually schedule afternoon classes, allowing me the freedom to sleep late every morning.

Having been raised in the transient environment of the Air Force, I had an advantage when it came to adapting quickly to new surroundings. I took full advantage of the parties which accompanied the first semester football season. Little by little, all of this hoopla about being an Aggie began to get to me. I soon found myself closely observing the activities of the Corps of Cadets, the select group of military students on campus I had heard about at Fish Camp. I gradually became envious of their camaraderie and involvement and came to the conclusion that it was the Corps that made Texas A&M unique, somehow different from all of the other universities. I perceived this single entity as the catalyst of the spirit and camaraderie for which Texas A&M was known.

I often found myself day-dreaming during class, imagining life within its ranks. At the same time, I wondered why anyone in his right mind would want to subject himself to the rigid environment these cadets were forced to adhere to. I quickly noticed a strong unity among its members — a unity that I envied. The Corps somehow seemed to be mysteriously intertwined with the university's history and tradition, and I had a strange desire to become a part of it all.

A turning point for me came late one evening as I was attending the final midnight yell practice of the year. Thousands of students and former students were packed into Kyle Field, the football stadium on campus, for the traditional midnight yell practice.

Marshall, one of my roommates, invited me onto the football field afterward and introduced me to a classmate of his. The classmate happened to be a "yell leader." He and four other male students, three seniors and two juniors, were assigned to lead some thirty thousand students in yells during each of the football games.

Marshall had informed me that the student body elected the yell leaders the previous year. The tradition had apparently begun decades earlier when the university consisted entirely of male cadets. The upperclassmen had forced the freshmen to perform skits during half-time of the football games. Of course, the upperclassmen enjoyed any opportunity to embarrass the "fish," as freshmen are called, and this was simply another opportunity to do so. Eventually, the team trainers, who wore white uniforms, began assisting the freshmen on the sidelines. The upperclassmen soon began chanting particular words or phrases associated with the actions performed by the fish on the field. Consequently, the position of yell leader evolved.

As the university grew, the positions became more prestigious, and the total number of yell leaders was eventually limited to five.

"Today, potential yell leaders have to campaign for a couple of weeks and compete in student elections to acquire one of the positions," Marshall said as we made our way through the mass of humanity toward the football field.

This particular evening was the final yell practice of the year and emotions reached the surface, as seniors in the Corps realized they would no longer be able to directly participate in this honored tradition.

As we made our way to the field, I looked back and was amazed at how many people had filled the stadium and had stayed until approximately one in the morning for its conclusion. The feeling of excitement intensified as we stepped onto the track under the bright light, glaring from atop the stadium. Chills ran up and down my spine as the Aggie Band pounded out the beat of its final number. I had never experienced anything quite like this before, and felt as if I were part of a huge movie set and at any moment an unseen director would holler "Cut! Okay, it's a take!"

As a young freshman, I could only imagine what it would feel like to be directly involved in an activity of this magnitude, much less to be leading it.

"If the environment of the Corps is so rigid," I thought to myself as we watched the spectacle, "then why does everyone seem to be having such a good time?" Something just didn't make sense. I couldn't figure it out.

I was introduced to the head yell leader that evening at the conclusion of yell practice and thought about the great opportunity he had before him. As several members of his outfit approached, he could no longer contain his emotion. Tears fell down his face as they embraced him, one by one. Some called him by his first name, others simply called him "sir." I presumed they had developed a very close relationship while participating in the Corps and were probably disappointed to see the yell practices end. The more I watched, the more I wondered what kind of experiences would make these grown men cry.

I lingered in the stadium long after most of the other spectators had left and observed this same yell leader with his date talking with several other members of the Corps, laughing and exchanging humorous stories about their experiences over the last several years. As hard as I tried, I had difficulty relating to this experience and wondered if I would ever feel such gratification.

"If I had only one wish," I thought to myself as I walked through the dark stadium tunnel leading out into the cool night, "it would be to one day stand in that yell leader's shoes and feel what he is feeling."

I wasn't sure why, and I hadn't the slightest notion how, but I knew that, at the least, I had to try ... and try I would.

C H A P T E R 2

WHY ME?

As my first semester came to a close, the urge to become part of the Corps of Cadets intensified to the point of submission. I finally made the decision to join, and sought out just how I was supposed to go about it. When I broke the news to my roommates, they responded with disbelief.

"You're crazy!" Marshall laughed.

"You'll have to cut all of your hair off," Dave said, "and you know what that means?"

"No, what?" I asked.

"You'll never get a date! Why would you want to do something like that?"

I really didn't know how to respond other than to say that I simply knew this is what I wanted to do. I no longer wanted to be on the outside looking in. I wanted to know what it felt like to be a part of the history and tradition of Texas A&M. I wanted to know what this spirit and pride was really all about; for I had never seen or felt anything like it before in my life.

The following day I walked into the Corps Headquarters and told the cadet behind the desk that I had come to join the Corps. He looked a bit flustered and said, "Just a minute, I'll get someone who can help you."

He returned with an older-looking cadet, obviously a senior, his knee-high riding boots with spurs giving him away.

"So," the senior began, "you want to join the Corps? Why would you want to do something like that?" Dejavu.

"I'm not really sure," I responded. "I just do."

After a brief conversation, he directed me to speak with one of the active duty military officers assigned to the university. After meeting with several of the officers, it was decided that, since I preferred the Air Force and was majoring in business, I should be assigned to squadron number two — a predominantly business outfit — after the Christmas break.

That afternoon I walked to the "quad," where the Corps dorms were located, to see if I could meet a few members of the outfit that called themselves the "Gators." As I passed through the arches at the north end of the quad, I sensed that my life had drastically changed.

A cadet who was passing by gave me directions to the dorm where Squadron Two could be found. Once inside, an experience that I will never forget then occurred. A string of short haired cadets were walking slowly in a single file line down the right side of the hallway. As they cautiously walked, I noticed their right shoulders remained up against the wall at all times. They stopped every two or three steps as if they were keeping watch for some unknown foe. Suddenly they looked my way and began slamming their bodies up against the opposite wall, yelling, "Howdy, Mister Lane, sir!"

I wondered if they had mistaken me for someone else when a voice suddenly bellowed out from behind, "Howdy, fish!" I quickly turned to see who had caused these freshmen to react in such a bizarre manner. A large silhouette walked toward me as I squinted, trying to adjust my eyes to the sun shining in through the window behind him at the end of the hall.

"Can I help you find someone?" he asked.

"Yes," I responded as I attempted to regain my composure. "I'm looking for Dale Lane."

"You've got him. What can I do for you?" he said.

"Well," I began, "I've joined the Corps and will be in this outfit next semester."

"Great!" he responded. "Hey, fish! Get down here and meet one of your new fish buds!"

Approximately fifteen cadets scrambled at his command and stopped in a single file line before me.

"I want you fish to whip out to this guy. He'll be one of your fish buds next semester."

One by one I met the freshman class of Squadron Two.

"Howdy, fish Probst is my name," the first cadet said as he held his hand out with his elbow at a ninety degree angle.

"Hi," I said. "I'm Dan." All the while, I was wondering if he had something wrong with his arm.

"Glad to meet you, Dan," he responded.

"Howdy, fish Roosma's my name. I'm glad to meet 'ya," the second one repeated in a similar manner.

"Howdy, fish Jumper's my name. Glad to meet you," the third one echoed. The remaining introductions deviated little.

As I looked into the eyes of these freshmen, I could see a form of discipline not often demonstrated in 18-year olds of my generation. Yet, at the same time it seemed as if they were somehow loving every minute of it. A small cadet by the name of fish Ogdee gave me a slight grin as he introduced himself to me. He seemed to be saying, "Are you sure you know what you're doing?"

I had the distinct urge to gather all of these freshmen into a room and quiz them about life in the Corps of Cadets. I wanted to say, "Come on, you guys, what's going on here? Do you guys really enjoy living this way, or are you just putting on a show for the rest of the school?"

As we finished the introductions, Dale Lane asked, "Play any sports, Quinn?"

"A few," I responded.

"Good. The Gators are known for sports around here. We'll see you after Christmas break. Come see me when you get back."

I left the dorm with a myriad of emotions. Did I really want to subject myself physically and mentally to this type of lifestyle?" I wondered. "Didn't I come to college to learn and enjoy myself? Dave was right. I'll never get any dates if I cut my hair as short as those guys. What are my parents going to say? What are my friends back home going to think?" I guess I would find out soon enough.

Christmas break seemed like an eternity back in Arkansas. My family was slightly perplexed as to why I had decided to make such a "drastic" decision. My father, an officer in the Air Force, had once visited Texas A&M as a high school senior while trying to decide which college to attend. He had once told me he simply didn't like the idea of someone only a year older than he was, telling him to get down and do push-ups. He opted on the ROTC program at East Texas State, instead. I suppose I really couldn't blame him for his rationale.

I spent many long nights over the next few weeks wondering what the next semester held in store for me. I wasn't sure how I would be accepted by the other freshmen in the outfit. They had obviously become a close-knit group and had already been through a lot together. I was determined to do all I could to gain acceptance as quickly as possible. I knew it wouldn't be easy, though, but sensed it would be worth it in the long run. I made up my mind that if I had to go through hell and back, then that's just what I would do!

When I returned to A&M for the spring semester my first stop was the barber shop. I didn't want my high school friends back in Arkansas to see me with my head buzzed, so I decided to wait until I got back to College Station. As large clumps of my hair fell to the floor, I realized I hadn't been shaved so close since I was a boy.

But it was too late to change my mind now. I left the barber shop amazed at how clearly I could now hear. I drove to my old apartment to bid farewell to my former roommates for the last time. They enjoyed teasing me about my haircut and took turns feeling the stubs on the back of my neck. They actually did give me some words of encouragement and invited me back as soon as possible. I said good-bye and headed to the main campus and a new way of life that would govern me throughout the next several years. I found a parking spot near the Corps dorms and walked to the quad. I passed several cadets who had gathered outside to share their Christmas break experiences with each other. Once I reached the dorm that would be my new home, I took a deep breath and entered. I went to Dale Lane's room. He was waiting to greet me and promptly introduced me to the outfit's first sergeant, a junior named Steve London. After a quick welcome, Mr. London took over and ushered me from room to room, introducing me to the outfit.

I met the seniors first. They seemed friendly enough and were all anxious to offer a few words of advice about surviving as a freshman in the Cadet Corps. Several began to say things like, "Do you know what a Zip is?"

"No, sir," I responded each time.

They would normally chuckle and say, "You will, but you had better keep it to yourself."

"Yes, sir," I said.

As we moved from room to room, I began to wonder why everyone was being so friendly to me. "This isn't going to be so bad," I convinced myself. "Maybe all of that discipline stuff is just for show. Things in the dorm must be more relaxed than I had imagined."

I was then introduced to the juniors. And they, too, seemed somewhat cordial.

The first one asked, "Ever heard of a surgebutt?"

"No, sir," I responded.

"Good," he laughed. "Let's keep it that way."

"Yes, sir," I replied again. I sensed they were playing with me, but couldn't figure out just what they were up to. The sophomores were next, and they were an entirely different story. When I met them, they let me know on no uncertain terms that they did not want to get too friendly with me. They demanded immediate respect from me — period. I was informed that it would be their job to break me and turn me into an Aggie. I wasn't exactly sure what that meant, but I had the distinct impression I would soon find out.

I was strongly encouraged to remove my high school letter jacket, for I was now an Aggie in the Corps of Cadets at Texas A&M. All of my high school accomplishments were in the past. I was to start over and would be required to earn the respect of other members in the Corps, not by my past achievements but by my future accomplishments. I got the impression that these "suggestions" were no longer optional.

I was told to forget about individuality because I was now part of a team that would require complete unity. Individual pride had no place here, only team pride mattered now.

"You got that, fish Quinn?" one sophomore asked in a stern voice.

"Yes, sir," I answered, having become accustomed to the routine.

"What's that, fish Quinn? I can't hear you," he said with a serious look.

"Yes, sir!" I repeated a bit louder.

"That's better," he replied, glancing up at Mr. London with a cocky grin. "Now, go hit the bag and get ready for tomorrow. You're gonna need all of the rest you can get. And, by the way, if you ever hear the word pisshead, you better not repeat it."

"Yes, sir," I replied. I left the room wondering why I had decided to do this to myself.

CHAPTER 3

IN TROUBLE ALREADY

I picked up my bags and followed Mr. London down the hall as he turned and opened a door on his right. "This will be your hole for a while," he said as we entered. "You won't be allowed to call it a room until next year ... that is, if you make it."

I learned quickly that every privilege in the Corps would have to be earned. The room was approximately 15 feet by 10 feet and came complete with a bunk bed, two desks and two chairs. No carpet or other furniture was allowed. The floors were tiled and windows were bare, with the exception of blinds.

A short, stocky cadet, who was sitting at one of the desks, snapped to attention when he saw us enter the room.

"Howdy, Mr. London, sir!" he shouted, his body erect.

"Howdy, fish Smiley," Mr. London answered. "This is fish Quinn. He's going to be your old lady this semester."

Smiley and I shook hands as Mr. London turned to leave. "Teach him everything you know," he said pulling the door shut behind him.

"You're probably wondering why my hair is so short," Smiley said as I began to unpack my bags.

"Yea," I replied, "it had crossed my mind."

"I'm on the Fish Drill Team."

"What's the Fish Drill Team?"

"We compete against other colleges in drill competitions. We have to keep our hair short for inspections. Someone out there thinks it makes us look sharp. Personally, I think it's just a pain in the butt."

As a member of the distinguished Fish Drill Team, Smiley was put through more than most cadets. During these drill competitions they often faced juniors and seniors from other colleges with several years of drill experience. The Fish Drill Team at Texas A&M practiced hours upon end each afternoon to perfect the flawless maneuvers for which they had become known. They had dominated the national championships held in Washington D.C. and had won all of the last five competitions. Many believe that was the reason the national competition had been discontinued.

Fish Smiley had me up at 5:30 the following morning to begin our preparation for morning inspection, a ritual that is conducted by the sophomores at the break of dawn. We were actually not allowed to rise for another half hour, so Smiley placed a towel at the base of the door to block the light from our desk lamps. Were we to get caught rising early, we would have both been in trouble.

I was soon taught that one of the few privileges allotted freshmen was to get away with anything he could, as long as he didn't get caught. This was all fine and dandy, but should a freshman get caught doing something wrong, his fish buddies would usually pay the price for the disobedience. This unique form of discipline had a tendency to be very effective. I concluded that peer pressure was the driving force behind the obedience process in the Corps. If a fish decided to break any rule, the entire freshman class was expected to be in complete agreement in advance. We were also expected to be in agreement as to why that particular rule was to be broken. This showed the upperclassmen that we were unified as a class, and worked together as a team. Unfortunately, it was very difficult to get everyone to agree on anything at this stage of the game.

At 6 a.m. a whistle blasted in the hallway, followed by the voice of a cadet bellowing out, "Fightin' Gator Two! First call for chow!"

"Who's doing that?" I asked as Smiley showed me how to prepare my uniform.

"It's one of your fish buds," he said. "That's the first call for morning chow. He's explaining what we're having for breakfast and which uniform we're assigned to wear today. It's one of our fish privileges. Don't worry, you'll get your turn."

This whistle blew three times, each in a distinct location of the hallway. Smiley continued to explain these "fish privileges." We were responsible for picking up and delivering laundry, delivering the daily newspaper, pulling senior boots off, and any other tedious assignment the upperclassmen could dream up.

At approximately 6:15, we began to congregate in a predetermined fish hole. This allowed time for the freshman class to look over each other's uniform prior to actually facing the sophomores for morning inspection. After a quick round of introductions, the freshmen began simultaneously cramming my mind full of rules and procedures as they glanced over my uniform with meticulous scrutiny.

"I wonder what kind of mood the pissheads are in this morning?" fish Lane asked the group as he stared at my name tag.

"I hope they're in a good mood," fish Garrett warned, "because Probst and Roosma are late again. Someone call them to see if they're even up."

I recalled the term "pisshead" from the previous night and wondered what the connotation actually meant.

"What's a pisshead?" I finally asked.

"That's a nickname for a sophomore," fish MacAnally responded, "but you don't know that word."

McAnally then explained that we weren't allowed to acknowledge several words as part of our everyday vocabulary. We weren't even allowed to acknowledge hearing them. The word "pisshead" was only to be spoken by the sophomore rank or higher. "Surgebutt," I was told, represented a junior, and could only be spoken or acknowledged by juniors and seniors.

The most sacred of all words was "zip." It stood for a senior and was only spoken or acknowledged by seniors. The slightest reaction when this word was spoken meant certain disaster for the entire fish class.

The previous evening's introductions began to make more sense to me now. Several upperclassmen had spoken these words, knowing I had not yet been briefed on their meanings. I was then informed that fish were not allowed to think, like, want, or feel. And I was warned that the upperclassmen would do their best, each day, to trick us into either saying or responding to one of these human emotions.

"You better be on your toes, Quinn," fish Jumper warned. "They'll try to trick you, knowing you're new and all."

Luckily, I was not the only new cadet in the room. Three other "frogs," as we were called, were present. The term "frog" was branded upon those of us who had joined the Corps after the first semester. Little did I know that only one of us would return the following year.

As the other freshmen looked over my uniform, they suddenly began to criticize fish Smiley for the job he did preparing me. "His shoes look like they've been shined with a Hershey's bar," fish Elmer lamented, pointing down at my feet.

"The brass on his uniform isn't shiny enough," fish Lane added.

"Look at all of the Brasso in the cracks of his belt buckle," fish Garrett said as Smiley's face slowly began to turn red.

"I didn't have time!" he said, defending himself. "He's only been here one night! What do you guys expect, miracles?"

The tension in the room was becoming uncomfortable, as my uniform seemed to have suddenly become the focus of everyone's attention. I had no idea that these morning inspections were so important. But, just as tempers were reaching a boiling point, our attention was diverted to the door. Two cadets entered, each scrambling to button his shirt as they stumbled over one another into the room. Their initial entrance reminded me of some old Dean Martin and Jerry Lewis movie.

"It's about time!" fish Smiley stammered, hoping to divert the conversation away from me. "What happened now?"

"Oh, Probst's alarm clock didn't go off again," the tall lanky one said with disgust.

"That ain't true," the other one responded. "It rang, but Roosma turned it back off. It's a good thing I've got my back up alarm clock strapped to my bunk or we might still be asleep and ..."

"Wrong!" the tall one responded, interrupting the other in mid-sentence.

"That's fish Roosma and fish Probst," Smiley whispered to me as I desperately tried to wipe the Brasso from the cracks in my belt buckle. "They're always getting us in trouble. We're thinking of putting them both in laundry sacks and dropping them off at the airport."

I wasn't in a position to make any judgments at the time, and continued to remove the Brasso from my belt buckle. My thoughts were still consumed with my uniform.

Suddenly, a voice from the hallway bellowed, "Get out here, fish!"

"Quick! Single file! Let's go!" fish Ogdee urged.

As we filed out of the room, Smiley whispered, "Just do what I do, and say as little as possible. Whatever you do, don't laugh. That's the ultimate insult to a pisshead."

We left the room, made a right turn, and were told to move up against the wall on both sides of the hallway. We were then commanded to look straight ahead. This was a freshman's ultimate torture because we were forced to look into the eyes of another fish standing directly across the hall. In order to resist the temptation to laugh, we tried to focus on the other's forehead, doing everything possible to avoid eye contact.

I noticed fish Roosma and fish Probst standing next to each other on the opposite side of the hallway. Fish Roosma seemed to lean into fish Probst every time a sophomore turned his back, obviously trying to get fish Probst to crack a smile.

"These two are bad news," I thought to myself. "If I hang around with them, I'll never make it through".

"Fish Quinn, do you think you could recite the first three campusology questions?" a rough looking sophomore suddenly asked.

"I don't think I know what a campusology question is," I responded with an obvious tremor of doubt in my voice.

"Oh, you don't think, do you?" he countered, glancing over at fish Smiley.

I could see fish Probst's eyes roll back into his head as he and Roosma turned pale.

"Is that one of your three authorized answers, fish Quinn?" he questioned again.

"I think so," I responded, not having the slightest idea what he was talking about. By now, I could sense the freshmen around me becoming tense, somehow preparing for the worst.

"Do you know who I am?" the sophomore continued as the rest of the sophomores began to laugh.

"No, sir."

"I'm Mr. Ingram," he continued, "and I don't think I like you very much, fish Quinn. How does that make you feel?"

I had the distinct feeling I was again being set up, when I suddenly remembered what I had been told earlier that morning about a fish not being allowed to think, like, want, or feel. Mr. Ingram had suckered me into acknowledging the human emotion of thinking, forcing me to break one of the cardinal rules we fish were never to break. As I contemplated how to answer his last question without getting into more trouble, I realized that another sophomore already had fish Smiley on the floor doing several push-ups for each of my mistakes.

"Answer me, fish Quinn," he continued, his voice changing to a lower pitch in mid sentence. "How does it make you feel?"

"I don't know, sir," I said with relief, knowing I was publicly not allowed to feel.

"Wrong answer," he said. Smiley was told to push again. "A fish has three answers and three answers only. They are; yes sir, no sir, and sir, not being informed to the highest degree of accuracy, I hesitate to articulate for fear that I may deviate from the true course of rectitude. In short, sir, I am a very dumb fish and do not know, sir. You think you got that, fish Quinn?"

"Yes, sir," I replied, this time with a slight tone of confidence. "Wrong again!" he said. This time, Smiley began to push without being told. "You ain't allowed to think, remember?"

I quickly began to calculate my odds of surviving this day, much less the rest of the semester. I surmised that if the pissheads didn't drive me insane, fish Smiley would probably kill me. Either way, I wouldn't be a very popular cadet.

I learned later that Mr. Ingram was a pisshead that apparently demanded immediate respect but, at the same time, had the reputation of being fair. I was informed that he had been a member of the Fish Drill Team the previous year and was now an advisor to the organization.

There were several historical questions about the university we were expected to memorize. And we were expected to do push-ups each time a slip of the tongue occurred, no matter how small or insignificant. It became my goal to memorize five campusology questions each week. There were 33 questions in all, and the other freshmen already had them committed to memory.

As we filed out of the dorm for morning formation, the freshmen began running with their hats held high over their heads while yelling at the top of their lungs. I followed suit, and ran to our designated location on the quad for morning formation. This tradition of yelling was

known as "wildcatting." I don't know how it began, but I imagined it
had something to do with the upperclassmen giving the fish another lesson in humility. Once in formation, we were to continue wildcatting
until told to "rest," which meant we were to be silent.

"Boy, am I glad my high school friends aren't here to see me doing
all of this," I thought to myself. "They'd never let me live it down."

Once in formation, we were instructed to stand at attention with our
chins tucked tightly against the front of our necks. Each hand was to be
clasped in a fist and pressed tightly against our sides. The heels of our
shoes were to be together with toes extended at a 45-degree angle.

A member of the Aggie Band then played "Reveille" on the trumpet,
announcing the beginning of formation. Meanwhile, the senior in
charge accounted for every cadet and saluted as "Call to Colors" was
played. These formations occurred prior to morning and afternoon
chow each day, come rain, sleet or snow.

A junior lead the outfit in a rhythmical chant called a "jody" as we
marched toward the chow hall. I watched in amazement as we entered
Duncan Dining Hall. Thousands of cadets scrambled to their tables to
prepare for the meal. The freshmen in my outfit instinctively began to
prepare several tables that were apparently reserved for us. There were
eight seats per table, each reserved for a specific cadet class. Seniors
were always seated at one end of the table with the juniors sitting next to
them. Sophomores were placed in the middle, while the freshmen were
seated on the opposite end of the table from the seniors.

This particular seating arrangement was devised for several reasons.
Freshmen were located near the isle, as it was our "privilege" to refill any
item of food whenever needed. This location gave us free access to the
aisle, allowing us to retrieve the needed food without disturbing the
upperclassmen.

The sophomores were seated next to us, keeping a close eye on our
every move. Juniors acted as a buffer between the sophomores and
seniors. Their primary responsibility during chow was to insure the
sophomores handled any problems, eliminating any possibility of the
seniors being disturbed while eating. Once the table had been set, we
stood at attention behind our chairs prior to being seated.

"Mr. Day, sir," Garrett began, "Fish Garrett requests permission to
ask a question, sir."

"Shoot," Mr. Day responded.

"Fish Garrett and fish Quinn request permission to be seated, sir."

I quickly learned that in order for a fish to ask a question, he needed to receive permission from an upperclassman to even ask the potential question. This seemed a little redundant to me, but felt it was no longer my place to question the unusual.

"You and the other fish can be seated, fish Garrett," Mr. Day responded, "Fish Quinn needs to learn to speak for himself."

I stood there in disbelief as fish Garret and the other two fish took their seats. I tried to recall the proper procedure for asking a question.

"Mr. Day, sir," I began. "I want to ask a question, sir." As soon as I had said the word "want," I received a look of terror from fish Garrett. I suddenly realized I had again screwed up. I had forgotten, fish were not allowed to want. I glanced to fish Jumper hoping to receive some assistance, but only saw my own mounting concerns reflecting in his eyes.

As the upperclassmen began to snicker, Mr. Day asked sternly, "Do you have brain damage, fish Quinn?"

I figured no matter how I responded to his question, it would only get me into more trouble. I decided at this point, silence was the best policy and remained at attention, saying nothing. Eventually, Mr. Lane intervened and allowed me to sit. Little did I know that an act as simple as eating was easier said than done as a fish in the Corps.

"Has everyone had firsts on the bullneck that would care for it, please?" Fish Garrett suddenly belted out.

"Yes, thank you!" fish Jumper and fish Neese answered in unison.

"Shoot the bullneck, please!" fish Garrett shouted.

"Shorts on the bullneck, please!" Jumper and Neese responded together.

I was receiving a crash course on the ritual freshmen had to perform in order to receive each item of food. What fish Garrett had done was ask if the upperclassmen had all been served the meat. The other freshmen at the table had surveyed the situation and had answered him, letting him know that all upperclassmen had indeed been served. By saying, "shoot the bullneck, please," he was asking for the meat. Once a particular type of food had finally reached a freshman's hand, the other fish could then receive the same item by simply saying, "shorts on the bullneck, please."

This procedure was repeated by the freshmen for every item of food on the table and, of course, every item was referred to by a nickname. Water was known as "sky." Milk was called "cow." Salt and pepper were referred to as "dirt and sand," or could be abbreviated by referring to it simply as "sand and." My personal favorite, mustard, was called "baby." If anyone wanted a piece of bread, they simply said "deal one, please." We would have to wait until we were seniors before we could "drop handles" with the food. Only seniors were allowed to refer to the food by its correct name.

Things occurred very quickly at chow, and I found the initial pressure intense. There was so much to learn and so little time. Very few freshmen, made it through both morning or evening chow completely unscathed. The high noise level in the dining hall only added to the confusion. It was easy to miss an important request with thousands of cadets shouting simultaneously.

During these meals we were responsible for protecting two items with our lives; our bider and the outfit guide-on. Biders were the hats we were required to wear with our cadet uniform. We sat on them while eating, keeping them out of the upperclassmen's reach. If an upperclassman were to steal a freshman's bider, the unfortunate cadet would usually be required to wildcat all the way back to the dorm and report to the upperclassman's room. In order for the fish to get his bider back, he would normally be required to perform some sort of exercise, like a class set of push-ups. For us, that meant eighty one.

The guide-on was our outfit flag. It was protected at all times by our entire freshman class. Should it be stolen, either by one of our own upperclassmen or by a member of another outfit, our entire fish class would be held accountable. An outfit without a guide-on, much like a fish without his bider, was ridiculed to no end by the rest of the Corps.

This particular morning, a scream of terror rang out from the middle of the chow hall. We turned to see a brave sole sprinting out the door with another outfit's guide-on. Close behind, an entire freshman class was in hot pursuit. He ran from the chow hall and was eventually caught and thrown to the ground by the freshman class. A loud "Whoop" was heard throughout the chow hall when the fish returned victorious with their guide-on.

As I began to eat my breakfast, I sensed Mr. Day surveying my

actions from the corner of his eye. I watched fish Garrett closely, looking for cues so I wouldn't do anything else wrong. He carefully cut his
eggs and swallowed a tiny bite from his plate and returned his fork to
the table. I wondered why he was eating such small bites and concluded
that he simply wasn't hungry. I could somehow sense something about
to happen as I picked up my biscuit and began to eat. I took a rather
large bite and began to chew while Mr. Day watched without blinking.

"Fish Quinn," he interrupted, "was that a fish bite?"

I put the biscuit down and instinctively returned to attention, wondering what I had now done wrong. I thought about the question and
concluded that, since I was now a fish and I had taken a bite, then it was
indeed a fish bite.

"Yes, sir," I answered, knowing full well no matter what answer I
gave him would probably be incorrect.

"Wrong!" he wailed. It was about this time that I concluded both
Mr. Day and Mr. Ingram had probably been severely deprived as children and had finally been given the opportunity to vicariously strike back
at their abusive parents through me.

"Don't you know how a fish is supposed to eat?" he asked as he
glanced over at fish Smiley who was sitting at the next table.

"No, sir," I responded, wondering if I was allowed to 'know.'

"Well, why don't you stop by my room after chow for a short lesson
in fish etiquette?"

"I can hardly wait," I thought to myself.

Eventually, the upperclassmen completed their breakfast and slowly
began to filter out of the dining hall. As the sophomores began to leave,
Mr. Brown instructed us to "chow down." This meant we could now
take normal bites for the last few minutes.

Everyone began eating like there would be no tomorrow, knowing
the privilege would not last long. Were it not for these "chow down"
periods, malnutrition would have easily swept through the entire freshman class of cadets within the first couple of weeks. Within seconds,
everything in sight had been completely engulfed. That's when the
belching contest began. Fish Roosma scored a perfect ten and won the
event, hands down.

We surrounded the guide-on and started back to the dorm, knowing
complete strangers might run past and snatch the flag and disappear into

a nearby dorm. I was warned that the upperclassmen in the Aggie Band loved to try to get fish to follow them into their dorm. Once inside, they would make the poor fish whip out to every upperclassmen in sight, leading the gullible freshman upstairs. They would normally end up on the fourth floor. I had heard horror stories of freshmen disappearing from the face of the earth in the band dorm, and I was taught to avoid it at all cost.

The Band members were referred to as "B.Q.s," or "Band Queers," by the rest of the Corps. They, in turn, referred to the other cadets as "C.T.s," or "Corps Turds;" an on- going rivalry between the two existed daily.

Each of us kept a watchful eye for anyone looking the least suspicious as we returned to our dorm. I received numerous words of wisdom from my new fish buds while walking back.

"You've got to take real small bites," fish Jumper warned. "They're called fish bites. That way your mouth will never be full when an upperclassman asks you a question."

"And you can only take one bite at a time," fish Adair added. "Between bites," fish Weinbaum interrupted, "you have to put your silverware back down and come back to attention while you chew."

Next, I was given advice on what to do when I returned to the dorm, since I had been directed to report to Mr. Day's room.

"Knock on his door three times," fish Ogdee said.

"Yea, three knocks lets let him know it's a freshman," fish Neese added.

I was told to wait outside until I was given permission to enter. Once inside, I was to place the tip of my shoes on the first tile crack in the floor and come to attention. Next, I was to greet each upperclassman in the room, beginning with the highest ranking sophomore. Since I didn't know Mr. Day's old lady, it meant I would have to whip out to him. After I had met his old lady and greeted everyone else in the room, I was to request permission to make a statement. Once approval had been given, I was to say, "fish Quinn reporting as ordered, sir." If I had made it that far, I was instructed by my fish buds simply to do as ordered.

"I hope you get out in enough time to help get our hole ready for morning inspection," fish Smiley said.

"Don't worry," fish Jumper consoled. "You won't do anything that the rest of us haven't done."

"Speak for yourself," fish Elmer remarked with a cocky sort of grin as we entered the dorm.

I was nervous about going into a sophomore's room, but had little choice at this point.

"Might as well get it over with," Garrett said.

"See 'ya in a few minutes," Smiley said with a false look of fear on his face, "assuming you survive, that is."

CHAPTER 4

PISSHEAD INITIATION

As we entered the dorm, the other fish immediately began greeting the upperclassmen by slamming their bodies up against the wall in recognition of the seniors' presence. "Hitting the walls," as it was called, was necessary when greeting seniors in the dorm. Most of the noise was made by the heels of our shoes as they slammed against the base boards.

Once each senior had been greeted by name, we began greeting the juniors. As the yelling continued, it became impossible to understand what was actually being said. Freshmen often took advantage of the confusion at these times and threw in some sort of cynical comment about one of the upperclassmen, hoping not to be heard through the noise. Once the greetings had finished, fish Neese, a quiet reserved freshman, tugged on my shirt sleeve and directed me to Mr. Day's room.

"Good luck," he said as he pointed, then disappeared into his hole with fish McAnally, his old lady.

I quickly tried to review the correct procedures for entering an upperclassman's room. I knocked three times on the door.

"Come in, fish Quinn," a voice from within echoed. I opened the door, looked down, and found the first crack in the floor tile. I came to attention and then looked up. I experienced a feeling of complete and absolute helplessness. The room was filled with sophomores.

"Well, fish Quinn, aren't you going to speak?" Mr. Day asked with an evil grin.

I felt like asking him to explain his abused childhood to me, but decided this was neither the time nor the place.

"Howdy, Mr. Day, sir!" I began. "Howdy, Mr. Ingram, sir!"

"Hold it right there," Mr. Day interrupted. "Mr. Ingram doesn't live in this room. You always speak to the two upperclassmen who live in the room first. Have you met my old lady?" he asked as he pointed to a guy who was leaning up against the bunk bed.

"No, sir." I said, realizing I had already forgotten some of my instructions.

"Well, whip out to him then." Mr. Day ordered.

I stepped over to the sophomore's right side as he leaned on his bunk, inattentively, cleaning his fingernails. I snapped my arm to a 90 degree angle and said, "Howdy, fish Quinn is my name, sir."

"Fish Quinn, Reese is my name," he slowly replied, returning my hand shake.

"I'm glad to meet you Mr. Reese, sir," I continued. "I'm from Gosnell Arkansas, sir. I'm taking Business Management, sir."

"Fish Quinn, I'm from San Antonio, Texas, and I'm taking Marketing."

"I'm glad to meet you, Mr. Reese, sir."

"I'm glad to meet you, fish Quinn."

This enlightening experience went on for the next 20 minutes as I moved from sophomore to sophomore, repeating my newly formed skill of whipping out. Once having met each of the sophomores, I was expected to memorize each by name and, eventually by home town and scholastic major. Mr. Day then informed me if I forgot any upperclassman's name, I would be expected to whip out again.

"You had better take off, fish Quinn," he suggested. "I'll talk to you later about your behavior this morning at chow."

"Yes, sir," I said with a silent sigh of relief.

I opened the door to leave. Mr. Day stopped me and said, "Hasn't Smiley taught you how to exit an upperclassman's room?"

"No, sir."

I was directed to again come to attention as I had done when I first entered. Then, I was instructed to ask permission to ask a question. Once permission had been granted, I was then allowed to ask for permission to "take off."

I repeated the instructions and received permission to leave. I walked out into the hall, turned right — making sure my right shoulder remained up against the wall— and began walking back to my hole. I figured the less time I spent in the hall, the better. I decided to increase my pace, hoping to avoid having to whip out to any more upperclassmen, and managed to get within three steps from my hole before being spotted.

"Hey, fish Jones," a voice pierced the silence from behind.

I hesitated, hoping there was another fish in the hall by the name of Jones.

"Fish Jones," the voice sounded again, "do I know you?"

I turned to see to whom the voice was directed. "Yea, you," a short cadet with senior riding boots said. "You had better bust butt down here and meet me."

"What choice do I have?" I thought to myself. "I guess I could just quit right now and go back to being a normal student."

I quickly erased the thought of quitting from my mind and ran to meet the senior. Just as I was about to whip out, Mr. Lane stepped from his room.

"Better let him get going. It's getting late and he needs to get his hole ready for inspection before class."

"I'll let you meet me later," the stranger said with a perturbed look on his face.

"Get on back to your hole, and don't stop to meet anyone," Mr. Lane said.

"Yes, sir," I replied with relief.

Fish Smiley was busy tucking in the sheets to his bed as I entered the hole. "Better hurry up," he said. "We've got 10 minutes to get this place ready for morning inspection before class."

"Are we inspected every morning?" I asked.

"Doesn't matter," he replied, as he began to wipe the blinds with a wet rag. "We've got to have our hole ready every day, just in case."

I began pulling the covers tightly across my bed, trying to remove any wrinkles caused from the previous night's sleep. Our beds were expected to resemble those in a hospital. We used a coat hanger to place a 45 degree crease in the sheet and blanket at each corner of the bed, then tucked it tightly underneath the mattress. The blanket and cover were rolled together at the head of the bed, then laid exactly 24 inches from the end with a six inch fold in the blanket. Each had to be measured perfectly, knowing the sophomores used a ruler during inspections. At night, we slept on a fitted cover sheet to eliminate having to remake the entire bed each morning.

Fish in Squadron Two were not allowed to have curtains on the windows and were expected to keep both the windows and blinds free of dust at all times. This posed a unique problem, however, because we were never allowed to look out of our window, even while cleaning it. We weren't actually privileged to look out of our hole at all, through the door or the window. Technically speaking, we could look at the window pane, but not beyond.

"If you get caught looking out of any window," fish Smiley advised, as he quickly wiped the dust from each individual blind, "you'll be sorry. If you're caught, your only hope is to try to convince the upperclassmen that you were only inspecting the dust on the glass. They won't have any way to disprove it."

"Do the rules ever end?" I asked.

"Not really, but you'll get used to it."

Our desks were also expected to be dust free, along with each of the three items allowed on it. Each shelf in the room was wiped clean, then items were returned and placed in descending order of height. Mirrors were wiped spotless, sinks were dried and plugged and, lastly, the floor was mopped prior to leaving.

Each closet had two bars for hanging clothes, the front for military uniforms and the rear for civilian clothes. Each piece of clothing was hung in a designated location, with all shirts and coats buttoned, pants zipped and snapped and coat hangers evenly spaced across the bar between one another. Shoes were placed under the bed, in specific order, with shoe laces tucked in. They were not allowed to extend from under the edge of the bed.

We glanced over the room one last time as we prepared to leave for class. "Better check to see if any dust has built up on top of the door," Smiley said.

"You've got to be kidding!" I exclaimed in disbelief.

"Nope," he replied. "Mr. Reese loves to gig for that."

"What's a gig?" I asked.

"It's a bad mark against you. Get enough of those and your life will be miserable."

"How could it get much worse than this?"

"You'll find out if you're not careful," he said as we headed to class.

Smiley surveyed the hall for upperclassmen as we left our hole and entered the hall.

"You'll eventually have to meet every upperclassmen on all four floors," he whispered as we headed toward the door. "You'll be expected to know each of them by name and speak to them whenever you see them."

"How many are there?" I whispered back.

"Around a hundred and twenty."

"That's it," I thought to myself. "I'm out of here. I'll quit after my morning classes. Yea, I'll just tell everyone that I'm allergic to fish Smiley, and I can't stay in the Corps because of an infectious rash caused by him."

I had whipped out to seven upperclassmen before we even got out of the dorm. Once outside, we were expected to whip out to any upperclassman who happened to be walking in the same direction. If they were ahead of us, we were required to catch up with them. If they were behind, we were to slow down and wait for them.

We were also to "sound off" while on the quad which meant we had to speak loud enough so everyone on the quad could hear us. We were told to speak to any upperclassmen we knew, no matter how far away they were. If a familiar upperclassman was walking with someone we didn't know, we were expected to whip out to the stranger, no matter how far we would have to run. Once off the quad, we were allowed to lower our voices and act somewhat civilized, as we would be among the regular university students.

I found it a mistake to walk with fish Smiley that morning. As a member of the Fish Drill Team, he had become familiar with many upperclassmen. I found myself whipping out to a new cadet every few seconds. In order to whip out while walking, we had to position ourselves to the right of the upperclassman and begin the introduction process while continually matching his stride and order of step. Rarely did they attempt to make it convenient for us.

Just prior to leaving the quad, a short, stubby cadet with shiny riding boots, pointed in my direction.

"Hey, fish Jones," he said, as he pointed at me. "What outfit are you in?"

"Why does everyone keep calling me fish Jones?" I asked Smiley. Before I received my answer, Smiley had already dropped his books and removed his bider. He quickly bent over into a crouched position and placed his hands on his knees.

"Fighting Gator Two!" he began as several other members in our outfit joined in. "The best! The boldest! The best damned outfit any-where!" He then concluded by wildcatting right there in front of several coeds who happened to be passing by.

"Oh, no," I thought. "I don't want to have to do that. Not in front of other people. Maybe I'll quit right now before someone calls me fish Jones again."

"What the heck was that all about?" I asked as Smiley placed his bider back on his head.

"Come on," he said with what little breath he had left.

"Let's get off the quad. I'll explain it to you later."

Three girls snickered as we quickly crossed the street in an attempt to get off the quad.

"Everyone has an outfit yell," Smiley explained. "Whenever a senior asks you what outfit you're in, you give him your outfit yell. Everyone else in the outfit, including the upperclassmen, have to join in, no matter where they are."

"Why does everyone keep calling me fish Jones?"

"That's just what upperclassmen call a fish they don't know," Smiley answered.

I began to look around for a hidden camera. I just knew someone was going to pop out of the bushes and tell me the last 24 hours was all a joke, and I was actually on Candid Camera. Unfortunately, it never happened.

The world returned to some semblance of normality once we were off the quad. Though we were still expected to speak to upperclassmen, our tone of voice was reduced. I entered my Geology class, found an inconspicuous spot amidst the two hundred students, and prepared for an hour of peaceful note-taking. Approximately 30 minutes into the class, I felt my eyelids begin to droop. The early morning uniform preparation had begun to take its toll on me. After several attempts to resist the temptation to doze off, the fatigue finally consumed me. I rested my head on my arm and quickly fell into a deep sleep.

Each student has his or her own fears about sleeping in class. My ultimate fear was to fall asleep, then wake to find the room empty and the lights off, knowing the entire class had silently left me in the room to finish my nap. On this occasion I awoke to the sound of books closing around me as students prepared to leave. I quickly arose, acting as if nothing had happened and exited the classroom somewhat embarrassed. It was unlike me to sleep in public, and I was now determined to get a good night's sleep in order to avoid any future humiliation.

Fish in the Corps of Cadets are expected to wear an immaculate uniform, free from wrinkle and stain. In order to keep the shirt tightly pulled down, we wore two thin elastic cords, interconnected around our waist. These elastic cords, called "boot straps," had a small hook on each of the ends. By connecting two boot straps together and wrapping them around our hips, we were able to tuck our shirt beneath them, giving our uniform a drum-tight appearance. Then, by rolling each side of our shirt, we would attempt to remove any possible wrinkle in front or back.

The front of the boot strap was usually placed under the groin area while the back was placed under the buttocks. This kept the boot straps from rolling up the waist.

I felt a sharp pain from my hips as I stood to leave the classroom. Recognizing a boot strap adjustment was in order, I exited the classroom and headed straight for the nearest rest room. To my surprise, two other fish had obviously encountered the same problem and were already making adjustments in front of the mirror. "These boot straps suck," one freshman exclaimed as I entered the rest room."

"Tell me about it," the other one responded.

"Isn't there a better way to do this?" I asked.

"If you find one, I'm in dorm seven, room 402. Come tell me about it," the first cadet responded.

I eventually tried everything from suspenders to a modified jock strap in order to avoid wearing boot straps. Nothing seemed to work as well. The suspenders, attached from the top of my socks to the bottom of my shirt, kept getting twisted up with the hair on my legs. The modified jock strap simply wasn't tight enough to keep my shirt down. I finally concluded that boot straps were the only alternative if I wanted to keep a respectable looking uniform, which in turn would help keep the pissheads off my back.

I somehow managed to overcome the urge to doze off during my next two classes and found myself with about 30 minutes to kill prior to meeting some of my new fish buds for lunch. After one more trip to the rest room for a final boot strap adjustment, I decided to stroll the campus for a few peaceful minutes.

The excitement of the new semester could be felt in the air as I watched hundreds of students hustling to get to class on time. The university felt like an entirely different place, now that I was part of the Corps of Cadets. The huge campus seemed like it belonged to me. I felt as though I had become heir to a part of history reserved for the few who wore the Aggie uniform.

As I strolled past the YMCA building, I imagined the yell leaders from long ago, chanting at midnight in unison with the rest of the Corps as the Aggie Band played the War Hymn. I began to actually feel as if I was part of the history and tradition of this honored institution. I felt a sense of belonging that I never thought possible at a school of this size.

Texas A&M was now my home. The Corps was now my family. The two became inseparable. I somehow knew that whatever I was about to experience would be worth every bit of sacrifice I would have to make.

I sat in the bleachers next to the drill field and envisioned the day I would march in my senior boots for the first time in Final Review. It seemed like an eternity away, and I wondered if I would ever actually experience it. Stories about all of the cadets that had either flunked out or quit were all too common.

"Would I actually feel the leather of the senior boots slip up and around my legs as I prepared for class as a zip?" I silently wondered. I instinctively looked around to make sure no one had heard me even think of the forbidden word.

I smiled, then realized that the thought of quitting had gradually slipped from my thoughts. I became excited about the challenges ahead. I realized this experience could either be torture or pleasure; it depended solely upon my attitude. I could enjoy it or hate every minute of it. I decided then and there to have as much fun as I could.

"After all," I thought to myself, "I'm not going to be here forever. Wasn't it all really just a game anyway? Wasn't it a freshman's privilege to get away with anything he could, as long as he didn't get caught?"

I took a deep breath and left the drill field with a renewed commitment. I decided to stick it out no matter what. As a matter of fact, I was going to enjoy every minute of it, whether the upperclassmen liked it or not!

C H A P T E R 5

MY FIRST
CRAP OUT

In nervous anticipation of the unknown, I arrived back at the dorm and gathered with several of the other freshmen in fish Probst's hole. There, we prepared for noon chow. Each cadet glanced over my uniform for any noticeable flaw, not wanting to take any chances with the Pissheads. They apparently knew the sophomores would seek every opportunity to find a minor imperfection in any of our uniforms.

We left the dorm and had no more taken three steps from the door when a senior across the quad yelled out "Hey, you fish! What outfit are you in?" For some unknown reason, fish Roosma yelled back, "Squadron Two! What's it to 'ya, sir?" The other fish stood there staring at fish Roosma in disbelief. Smiley was in complete shock, and Garrett looked like he wanted to tear fish Roosma's head off.

Fish Jumper looked at Roosma without focusing, his mind retreating into it's own private compartment where he was already visualizing the consequences of what had just occurred.

"I don't think that was the right answer," I whispered to Roosma as the senior quickly turned and began walking towards us.

"Pull out day, is it?" the senior asked as he began writing down our names from off our name tags. "You guys must have had a good Christmas break. Thanks a lot," he said as he finished writing down each of our names and began to walk away. "I can guarantee, you won't have a nice day."

"What's your problem, Roosma?" Smiley hollered in disgust.

"I just had a wild hair and felt like pulling something out," Roosma replied with a slight grin. "Don't worry, you guys. He was probably just bluffing anyway," he attempted to console. It was obvious no one else was buying it.

"You don't ever pull anything out without all of us approving it first!" fish Garrett wailed.

Fish Jumper looked distressed and paused for a moment, then muttered almost inaudibly, "I guess we can kiss weekend privileges goodbye for a while."

We were never supposed to independently break the rules or "pull out" privileges. Were any rules to be broken, the entire freshman class was to be in complete agreement first. It was supposed to show the sophomores that we had learned to place our fish class before ourselves.

We entered the dining hall wondering how long it would take for the news to spread about the incident that had just occurred. It didn't take long for the answer to come. Mid-way through our meal I noticed several upperclassmen whispering across the dining hall while glancing periodically in our direction. Suddenly, Mr. Brown slid his chair back and began to walk toward us.

"Don't look now," I said, "but that red headed sophomore looks like he's on his way over here." We dropped our utensils and came to attention.

"Howdy, Mr. Brown, sir!" we said in unison as he approached. It was fairly easy to tell when Mr. Brown was upset. His neck would turn a deep shade of red and his eyes became slightly bloodshot. Both were evident now. As he stood and looked at Roosma, all he said was, "Five o'clock. Sweats, combat boots, and rain gear. Everybody. Pass it on to the rest of your fish buds."

As he turned to walk away, Smiley looked at Roosma and whispered, "Thanks a lot, fish bud."

"What did Mr. Brown mean by that?" I asked as we began to eat again.

"Crap out time," Jumper answered. "We're gonna have a little physical exercise at five o'clock today. We have to wear our sweat suits, combat boots and rain gear," he continued.

"Why rain gear?" I asked. "The skies are clear."

"That makes you sweat more when you do push ups in the bathroom while they run the steam showers," Fish Ogdee responded. "It's loads of fun. Just wait."

The remainder of the meal was eaten in silence as each envisioned what would happen that afternoon.

"Come on, guys," Roosma finally said. "Crap outs are no big deal. All we have to do is act like we're tired right from the start, and they'll feel sorry for us."

"Speak for yourself," fish Neese said. "I don't like crap outs one bit."

As we were leaving the chow hall, Mr. Ingram was entering. He gave us one of his I-don't-like-you-anymore looks and said, "Why don't you fish wildcat all the way back to the dorm, just for the fun of it." We immediately removed our biders, raised our arms and ran back to the dorm, yelling at the top of our lungs. Needless to say, fish Roosma didn't win any congeniality awards that day. Roosma was a tall, lanky cadet whose father had been in the Corps years before. He was some-what mellow and carefree, which at times tended to test the patience of the other, more serious freshmen. Some cadets took the rigid environ-ment within the Corps very seriously and tried to avoid any potential conflicts with the upperclassmen. Others took almost every opportunity to test the waters.

It was not an easy task to mesh the diverse personalities into a unified freshman class, but that's what we knew we had to do. At times we were at each other's throat. Other times, we were elated. We knew that one day we would look back and realize we'd accomplished the task but, for now, we were simply trying to survive each day at a time.

Not really knowing what to expect, I was a little apprehensive about this form of discipline known as a "crap out." I found it difficult to con-centrate during my afternoon classes, knowing I would probably be sore for the next several days. I couldn't help wondering what the Pissheads were going to do with us. Tarring and feathering had gone out of style in Texas several years earlier. I remembered how in the old John Wayne movies they would drag the culprits behind horses through the sage brush in order to whip them into submission. I knew that such disci-pline would not be good for Corps publicity, so, I figured they would probably just make us do a few push ups and, if Roosma seemed truly repentant, that would be the end of it. I was wrong.

At 4:50 p.m., we gathered in fish Ogdee's hole to prepare for the crap out. Each fish had donned sweats, combat boots and rain gear as ordered. The atmosphere reminded me of a crowded locker room just prior to a big football game, with one big difference: no one really want-ed to be there. We anticipated the challenge ahead and tried to calm our nerves by cracking a few pisshead jokes.

"I hear Mr. Reinburg — who was part Indian — is on the war path today," fish Neese said.

"Yea, he had buffalo tongue for noon chow," fish Lane laughed.

"I wonder if Mr. Day used Scope this morning," Smiley began. "The last time he hollered at me, his breath almost made me pass out."

The jokes really didn't seem to help much. There were four of us in the room that had never been crapped out before.

"You frogs just try to do what we do," fish Smiley advised. "And don't worry, they're not allowed to touch you. It's against the rules. All they can really do is yell, so just let it go in one ear and out the other."

"Yea, that's real easy for Probst to do, cause there's nothing between his ears anyway," Roosma added while pushing Probst down on the bunk bed. Probst jumped up and punched Roosma on the arm and said, "You're the reason we're getting crapped out, Roos! Maybe you better watch it or we'll put you in a duffle bag and drop you off at the airport!"

"I'm scared," Roosma responded sarcastically.

"What's going on in there?" a voice yelled from the hall.

"Hurry up and get out here! Ten push ups for every second you're late!" someone else hollered.

"Let's get it over with," fish Weinbaum said as we headed toward the door.

Roosma must have pinched Probst in the butt as we were leaving the room because Probst let out a wail as we entered the hall. Roosma then snickered.

"Everyone drop and give me a class set!" Mr. Ingram demanded.

"What's so funny, fish Roosma?" Mr. Coffman asked. Roosma remained silent knowing whatever he said would only get him into more trouble.

We began our first class set of push ups, but were stopped several times for not counting together in unison. After several attempts to get to eighty-one, my arms began to ache.

"Get up against the wall!" Mr. Tevis finally ordered. We lined up against the wall, shoulder to shoulder, grateful for the opportunity to catch our breath. Mr. Tevis then lectured us as to why we were getting crapped out. We were reminded about teamwork and unity.

"When one fish screws up, everyone gets it!" he hollered. "You guys have to learn to work together as a team! You can learn it the easy way or the hard way, it's up to you!"

"That's right! Mr. Reed added. "Today you're going to learn it the hard way! Everyone drop again and push until I get tired!" After another attempt to complete a class set, we were told to "catch butterflies." This was a most unusual test of endurance.

We were to lean up against the wall and crouch to a sitting position. Our legs were to remain bent at a 90-degree angle with arms outstretched, grasping with our hands. This was to simulate our attempt to catch butterflies. For some reason, this was Mr. Hale's favorite exercise. He seemed to enjoy the agony on our faces as we attempted to keep our arms raised and legs bent. After about three minutes in this position, I began to discover several new muscles in my legs that I never knew existed.

I became aware of the distinct sound of water running from the bathroom down the hall. Steam began to slowly seep into the hallway from under the bathroom door while several of the pissheads began to head down to the bathroom.

"It's show time!" Mr. Goff announced.

"To the showers!" Mr. Cain yelled as several of the other sophomores joined in. "Move! Move! Move!"

We scrambled down the hall and crowded into the steam-filled bathroom and were immediately told to drop for more push ups. We each jockeyed for position, as floor space was at a premium.

"Class set!" Mr. Dugat yelled. "Go!" We began to push, but were again interrupted.

"Stop!" Mr. Reese yelled. "You guys aren't counting together. Start over!"

We continued to push as the steam continued to fill the room with a hot, dense mist — making it somewhat difficult to see. This began to remind me of wrestling practice in high school as sweat puddles formed beneath me while exercising.

"Up against the walls!" Mr. Hale ordered. "Start catching those *#@!*@#! butterflies!" I placed my back against the wall between two urinals. The steam was so thick I could barely make out the figures at the other end of the bathroom not more than ten feet away. The sweat suit beneath my rain coat was now soaking wet and becoming heavy. The rain gear I wore restricted the ventilation and made it feel as though I carried an extra ten pounds of water weight.

I could see other faces covered with sweat as they struggled to keep the proper butterfly position. I glanced over at Roosma and remembered what he had said at lunch about pretending to be exhausted early so the sophomores would feel sorry for us. His face seemed to express extreme agony but, with a wink and a slight grin, I knew it was mostly show.

I suddenly envisioned my former roommates off-campus, enjoying a lazy afternoon after class. They were probably watching a movie while sipping on some cool drinks. They would surely think I was insane if they could see me now. I had played various sports in high school and was somewhat accustomed to physical exercise, but the "steam shower" crap out was an entirely different experience. It was more a test of self control than anything else, as I tried to ignore the sophomores who were yelling at me from only inches away from my nose. I kept reminding myself that it was all just a game and, if I could just hang on a little longer, it would soon be over.

One of the freshmen suddenly became nauseous and darted to a nearby urinal to throw up. It was too close for me. I quickly moved across the bathroom to escape the odor. Suddenly, we were told to exit the showers and form up on the wall in the hall.

A blast of fresh air from the open door dispersed the stale smell of humanity and heat as we filed out of the bathroom. The look of misery on each freshman's face seemed to express genuine repentance, though I'm sure the sophomores questioned our sincerity. We eventually became fairly proficient at depicting penitent fish, especially during crap outs. We knew our saving grace, however, was the clock. Sooner or later we would be required to prepare for evening chow, and no crap out was allowed to interfere with meals.

Once we had lined up on the wall, Mr. Reinburg asked, in a rather perturbed voice, "Do you fish know why you just got crapped out?"

"Yes, sir!" we yelled together.

"One of you thinks he is above the rules." With the word "think" being mentioned, we immediately began our fish response indicating we were not allowed to think.

"You've got to learn to be united so we don't have to crap you out every day," Mr. Reinburg interrupted. "Everyone get down into the push up position, except for fish Roosma. Fish Roosma, you stay standing. The rest of you give me one more class set of push ups and then, in unison, tell fish Roosma thank you."

We dropped, and with every ounce of energy left, attempted one more class set of push ups. No one was actually able to complete it, so we simply tried to make it look good. When we were done counting, we said in unison, "Thank you, fish Roosma!"

"I don't think he heard that," Mr. Coffman said.

"Better tell him again."

"Thank you, fish Roosma!" we yelled again. It was hard to tell whether Roomsa really felt bad about what he had done or not, but the peer pressure within the Corps was enough to make a fish either want to straighten up or ship out, real quick.

Once the crap out was over, nothing more was to be said about the incident, either by the freshmen or the sophomores.

"Are you guys going to work as a team?" Mr. Ingram asked. "Yes, sir!" we responded.

"I couldn't hear you!"

"Yes, sir!" we repeated at the top of our lungs.

"What class are you guys?" Mr. Tevis asked.

"Class of eighty-one, sir!" we hollered with pride.

"Say it again so everyone in the dorm can hear you," Mr. Dugat ordered.

"Class of eighty-one, sir!" we again yelled with an intensity that seemed to rock the foundation of the dorm.

"You guys have 20 minutes to shower and get ready for evening chow. Now, move!"

We scampered to our holes as quickly as possible, relieved that the ordeal was over. While preparing for the shower, I was again reminded that a fish had to earn each privilege, no matter how small. We were required to wear slippers and a robe to the shower and were only allowed to carry a towel and a bar of soap. Were we to have anything else in our possession, it would mean another lesson in discipline.

Our time in the shower was limited to five minutes, no more. It was also not permissible for any of us to allow any visible steam to build up while showering. Were we to do so, it would be considered a steam shower, which was reserved for juniors and seniors only.

Showering in the Corps was not without its own particular dangers. If someone were to flush one of the toilets while the shower was running, it would divert the cold water from the pipes, making the water in the shower scolding hot. In order to avoid burning someone, the word "crapper" was yelled as a warning prior to anyone flushing the toilet. Those in the shower would respond with "shoot" prior to the toilet being flushed, allowing time for everyone in the shower to move from the path of the hot water.

On this particular afternoon, I was in the shower with several other guys, including Mr. Day. I noticed fish Probst enter the bathroom. From my position I was the only one in the shower who could see him. He gripped the toilet handle and glanced my way with one of his "dare me?" expressions. Mr. Day had his face buried beneath the stream of water and was unaware of what was about to happen. I nodded my head in agreement and stepped to the side, motioning to the other freshmen to do the same. Probst flushed the toilet without saying a word. A scream of pain echoed from the shower as Mr. Day jumped backwards, slipping on the wet shower floor. It was all we could do to keep from laughing, but somehow managed to hold it in while acting as if we had been burned also.

Probst scurried from sight and managed to disappear into his hole before Mr. Day could determine who the culprit was.

"Did anyone see who did that?" Mr. Day screamed as he scrambled from the shower, trying to regain composure.

"No, sir!" we answered.

"When I catch whoever did that, you're dead!" he yelled down the hall, sticking his head out the bathroom door while still dripping wet.

Whenever a fish got away with such an insignificant act, it tended to boost our morale. The instigator was, of course, either a hero or an outcast, depending upon whether or not the sophomores ever caught him.

Preparation for evening chow was almost identical to that of morning chow. We again buffed our shoes, polished our uniform brass, ironed our pants and shirt, then quickly brushed up on a few campusology questions prior to "falling out" into the hall.

Fish Neese called out the menu and uniform of the day from the hall, indicating we had five minutes to finalize our preparation. Again, we met as a class in a predetermined hole and inspected each other for any possible uniform discrepancies.

It was easy to detect the fatigue on the faces of the other cadets as, one-by-one, they entered the hole. It had been a long day for us, and I was already looking forward to getting to bed. Again fish Probst and fish Roosma entered late, chuckling about what had happened only moments before in the shower.

"Do you guys do things like that often?" I asked fish Probst as he wiped a speck of dust from Roosma's name tag.

"Every chance we get," he responded.

"Yea, and you're going to get us all in trouble, too," fish Elmer warned.

"Let's go. We don't have time to argue about this," fish Smiley remarked as we lined up toward the door.

We entered the hall as fish Neese was blowing the whistle for the second call. I felt something scuff my shoe as we turned to take our place on the wall. I had a feeling I had scratched the shine from the toe, but was afraid to look down. As I took my spot on the wall, Mr. Goff immediately asked me to recite the "Twelfth Man" campusology question. Luckily, it was one I had studied between classes earlier that day.

"Sir," I began as he proceeded to inspect my uniform, "In 1922, in Dallas, during a football game against Center College, an Aggie was called from the stands to suit up as a substitute. Hence the phrase, Twelfth Man, sir."

During my recital, Mr. Goff had noticed the smudge on my right toe.

"Fish Smiley," Mr. Goff said, "Is this your old lady?"

"Yes, sir!" Smiley replied.

"Did you teach him how to shine his shoes?"

"Yes, sir" Smiley again answered, this time with increased confidence.

"What did you use, sand paper?"

"No, sir!" I could feel it coming.

"Why don't you drop and give me a class set for not having your old lady ready for inspection," Mr. Goff ordered.

"Yes, sir!" Smiley obediently replied as he dropped to the floor.

As Smiley began to push, I had the distinct feeling we would not be rooming for long.

"One, sir! Two, sir! Three, sir!" fish Smiley counted as I listened helplessly.

"Why didn't you shine your right shoe?" Mr. Goff asked me.

"Mr. Goff, sir," I began, "Fish Quinn requests permission to make a statement, sir."

"Go ahead."

"I accidentally scuffed it as I was walking out of the door, sir."

"Quit pissing on my leg, Quinn," he said as the other sophomores began to chuckle. I had never heard this term before and wondered what was so amusing about it. Later I found out that it meant I was making up an excuse. I should have simply responded with one of my authorized fish answers, like "No excuse, sir."

Fish Smiley finished his push ups as we began to leave the dorm in a single file. As he glanced my way, I noticed the veins in his neck protruding. They pulsated rapidly as his heart raced from the push ups. We again wildcatted as we ran to our place in formation.

I watched intently as Mr. Tevis took his place at the front of the outfit with the guide-on and wondered what it would take to become the guide-on bearer next year. It appeared to be a prestigious position for a sophomore to hold, and I decided then and there that I wanted it.

At the conclusion of formation, we marched to chow. We entered Duncan Dining Hall and again the freshmen immediately began to prepare the tables. I was able to assist this time, having seen it accomplished during morning chow.

I was determined to avoid any possibility of chastisement during evening chow and was careful to cut my food into tiny bites prior to eating them. The pissheads again watched our every move, looking for any opportunity to put us in our place. I also made sure I sat securely on my bider, keeping it out of the reach of the upperclassmen.

Not yet familiar with the nicknames of the food, I waited for another fish to ask for each item. I then simply joined the other freshmen when they asked for "shorts" on each one. After a few minutes, I decided to redeem myself from morning chow. I noticed a bowl of pinto beans had been used and asked for permission to refill them. After acquiring permission, I handed my bider to fish Lane for safe keeping. I then slid my chair out from the table and began to walk away.

"Fish Quinn, do you think you're a senior or something?" Mr. Black said.

"No, sir," I responded, not understanding the question.

"It's only a senior's privilege to leave his chair out from the table, and by the way, you're not allowed to think either!

"This is going to be a long semester," I thought to myself. Luckily, Mr. Lane was seated at the table.

"We'll allow you to slide this time, fish Quinn," he said. "Just push your chair in, and we'll act like it didn't happen."

"Fish Smiley," Mr. Lane hollered, "would you brief your old lady on senior privileges at chow?"

"Yes, sir!" Smiley answered from several tables away.

I returned with a bowl full of pinto beans, just as a group of girls entered the dining hall. They were apparently part of a local sorority and carried a huge banner advertising an upcoming dance. Whistles and cheers filled the chow hall as they paraded through.

"Fish Jumper," Mr. McCan, a senior, yelled. "Go kiss one of those girls."

Fish Jumper sat there in disbelief. He apparently could not bring himself to obey the order. Seeing the opportunity to gain acceptance, I looked at Mr. McCan with an expression indicating I would fulfill the mission if asked.

"All right, fish Quinn," he said, "you go." I immediately rose from the table, remembering to push my chair in this time, and headed toward the female visitors. He grabbed my sleeve as I walked by and whispered, "Make sure you give her a good one."

"Yes, sir," I said.

I followed the girls to the front of the chow hall where they were displaying their banner for all to see. I politely tapped one of the girls on the shoulder. As she turned to see who it was, I said, "Excuse me. I've been ordered to kiss you." I then proceeded to accomplish my mission, slightly bending her backwards in the process. Not really knowing what had happened, she turned red. I'm sure I did the same. I thanked her and began to return to my table.

By now the entire chow hall was going crazy with cheers of approval. Amidst the clamor, I noticed Mr. Manley, a senior from the Group Staff table, attempting to head me off. I cut between two tables in an attempt to avoid the encounter, but to no avail. He caught me by the back of my belt and began to chew into me like I was his dinner that evening.

"What in the hell do you think you're doing, fish Quinn?" he hollered above the noise.

"Sir," I began, "Fish Quinn requests permission to make a statement, sir."

"What!" he responded impatiently.

"A fish is not allowed to think, sir," I answered. "Ha!" I thought. "I got him!" Unfortunately, he wasn't the least bit amused.

"Shut up!" he said with disgust. "I can't believe you did that! Do you know what you just made the Corps look like? Report to my room after chow!"

Mr. McCan interrupted him and tried to defend me by explaining that it was he who had given the order. Mr. Manley wasn't in any mood to listen.

"Don't worry," Mr. McCan told me as I finally took my seat. "He's just blowing smoke. He's probably just had his bootstraps on too long."

Everyone at the table laughed. All I knew was that I had apparently gotten myself into a big mess.

I reported to Mr. Manley's Group headquarters room that evening after chow and received a lengthy lecture on how I had degraded the reputation of the Corps of Cadets to a new, all time, record low. I was informed that we were to be gentlemen at all times and we were never, under any circumstances, to take advantage of young ladies in that manner.

"I should have you thrown out of the Corps for that, Quinn," he said. "You're lucky you're new, or I'd have your butt. I'm gonna give you three Rams for your behavior this evening. Mr. McCan gets three also. You two can spend the weekend together working them off. I'll be watching you from now on, so you had better be on your best behavior. Got that?"

"Yes, sir," I responded.

"Good. Now, get out of here and remember, I've got my eye on you."

Surprisingly, I received somewhat of a hero's welcome that evening when I returned to the dorm. Everyone wanted to know what had happened at Mr. Manley's room.

"Well, you're still alive," Smiley said. That's a good sign."

"I ain't believing you did that," fish Roosma remarked. "You're all right, Quinn," fish Probst added.

I tried to act like the entire incident was no big deal, but I hadn't yet gotten completely over the scare. I'm sure most of what Mr. Manley said was just a bluff, but he had gotten my attention. No one could believe Mr. Manley had rammed one of his own classmates. Mr. McCan was extremely upset about having to work off his rams over the weekend.

"From now on," I said to Jumper, "whenever I do something like that again, I'm going to make sure I don't do it in front of the entire Corps."

"You're learning, Quinn," Jumper said with a grin. "You're learning."

LATE NIGHT EXCITEMENT

O nce the commotion from my little excursion had ended, it was time to prepare for Call to Quarters, or "C.Q." as it was better known. During this period, from 7 p.m. to 10 p.m. each week night, freshmen and sophomores are required to be at their desks studying. No Corps related activities are allowed during this time. Initially, I looked forward to this period, thinking it would force me hit the books. Unfortunately, I was so worn out from the day's activities I found it difficult to keep from dozing off, which was also against the rules during C.Q.

A designated junior randomly inspected each hole throughout the evening to insure we were indeed at our desks studying. Each hour we received a five minute break and at 10 p.m. we were given 30 minutes to shower and prepare our uniform for the following day. All lights had to be out by 10:30 p.m. Just prior to retiring for the evening, Smiley and I would place our form fitted sheets over our beds, then crack a few jokes about the Pissheads before falling asleep.

As time progressed, I slowly became accepted among the Gator fish class. I even managed to work my way into a starting guard position on our fish basketball team. The Corps has an extensive intramural sports program and we were determined, as a freshmen class, to win the fish Corps sports flag. The flag is awarded annually to the freshman class with the most athletic points, overall, in the university's intramural program. For each sporting event, a certain amount of points is given, in several categories, to each cadet or team. At the end of the year, the team with the most points wins the flag.

Our toughest competition was from a Navy outfit known as E-2. This outfit consisted of various university athletes, many on athletic scholarships, who had decided to become part of the Corps of Cadets as well.

Our rivalry became fierce, and it often came down to our two outfits fighting for the championship in each sport.

We ended up winning the freshman championship in basketball and eventually did go on to win the top sports flag award in the Corps. Mr. McCan, the outfit athletic officer, went so far as to rent a tuxedo for our championship basketball game.

The entire outfit became involved in our success, and the excitement over our quest for the fish sports flag relieved some of the tension between us and the sophomores. And because of our athletic accomplishments, the seniors allowed us numerous additional privileges throughout the year.

After just a few weeks, I had somehow found the time to memorize most of the required campusology questions and was told by some of the upperclassmen that I had the potential to become a "sharp" fish. Actually, I had simply learned to play the game and enjoy myself. I tried not to take any of the pisshead harassment personally.

I realized that when it got really tough, the sophomores were simply trying to keep the juniors and seniors off their backs. By provoking us into doing something stupid, they could discipline us, and prove to the rest of the upperclassmen that they were indeed doing their job.

But we weren't entirely at the mercy of the sophomores. When push came to shove, we did have our own ways of striking back. Probst was known to have put heel and sole, a black liquid used on shoes, atop the toilet seats in the rest rooms. The liquid had a tendency to burn the skin, thus, from time to time, a sophomore would get caught with his pants down, so to speak, and end up with a hot seat.

Another method of retaliation was the dreaded "douche out." If we, as a freshman class, felt that one particular sophomore was being unfair with us, we could acquire permission from the first sergeant, a junior, to douche out the sophomore. It usually meant throwing a bucket of water — though I know of occasions when the liquid consisted of more than just water — on the victim late at night while he was asleep in his bunk.

A douche out could be a humiliating experience for a sophomore and, because they were such easy late night prey, we had to be sure our cause was justified. In actuality, a douche out was done more out of respect than anything else. We simply wanted to send a message that we were a bit tired of their strictness.

Once we had obtained a consensus among the entire freshman class that Mr. Ingram was in need of just such a lesson, We notified Mr. London, our first sergeant. He, in turn, secretly notified the junior and senior classes. There were always several juniors and seniors who wanted to witness the event.

At approximately 20 minutes past four, we quietly met in Fish Ogdee's hole to prepare.

"Shhhh! Listen up," Fish Smiley whispered, "everybody know what to do? Quinn, are you sure you want to be in on this, being new and all?"

"Yea," I said. "I don't think they'll suspect me."

"It's your decision," Smiley continued. "Your job will be to get the door open without making any noise. I'm going to toss the water on Mr. Ingram. Adair, you're going to put the stick on the door once I'm out of the room, and I mean out of the room."

"I still don't know about this," Fish Weinbaum said with a shudder. "Mr. Ingram gives me the creeps."

"Relax," Fish Roosma told him. "I've got a back up plan."

"What is it?" I asked.

"I ain't saying, but it's sure to confuse the pissheads."

A douche out was a performance that had to be orchestrated perfectly in order to be successful. Three designated freshmen were pre-selected to be the primary participants; one opened the door, another threw the water, and the third shut the door, then placed a specially cut stick on the outside door knob, wedging the door shut. If all went well, the stick would lock the sophomores inside of their own room. Only a junior or senior in the outfit was allowed to remove the stick from a door. After the stick had been placed on the door, we would then scramble back to our holes and hope the stick would hold until morning formation. After 6:30, no repercussions from the sophomores were supposed to occur.

I had volunteered to be one of the three, hoping the sophomores wouldn't suspect me. I also felt like getting involved in some late night excitement, hoping it would help solidify my place within the fish class.

One of the inherent risks of participating in a douche out was the possibility of being caught and getting crapped out until the first call for morning chow — which occurred at 6:30 a.m. If Mr. Ingram did escape from his room, he would be given three guesses to chose the three fish who directly participated. Only the first sergeant had the three names.

Were he to correctly guess one of the three, the individual selected would receive the crap out. If two of the three choices were correct, the two choices would both receive the punishment. If all three individuals who participated in the douche out were correctly chosen, the entire freshman class would be crapped out for two hours that morning. For this reason, it was very important that our class be in complete agreement before a douche out was even attempted. Everyone eventually agreed to being crapped out if Mr. Ingram successfully picked Smiley, Adair and I as the participants.

We left Ogdee's hole and quietly tip-toed out into the hall. To my surprise the hall was filled with juniors and seniors who wanted to watch the event. Smiley, Adair and I silently huddled outside of Mr. Ingram's door as the rest of the freshman class looked on nervously. Smiley quietly counted to three. I slowly turned the knob, trying not to make any unnecessary noise. Once the door had opened, I gave it a sharp push, causing it to slam up against the inside wall. Smiley quickly stepped inside and threw the water in the direction of Mr. Ingram who had been fast asleep on the lower bunk bed. A shriek was heard throughout the dorm as the water hit with a splash! Apparently, just as Smiley had released the water, Mr. Ingram had awakened and was already lunging toward him.

As Smiley attempted to turn and run from the room, Mr. Ingram managed to grab the back of his shirt, tearing part of it from his back. Smiley pounced from the room as Adair slammed the door shut. Adair then frantically scrambled to wedge the stick on the door knob as Ingram began pulling from the inside.

"It's on!" Fish Adair yelled. "Let's get out of here!" We all scampered back to our holes, hoping the stick would hold till morning.

Smiley and I jumped into our beds and pretended to be asleep, knowing it probably wouldn't be long before we would be rudely interrupted. I could hear Mr. Ingram pounding and shaking his door in an attempt to knock the stick loose. Suddenly, our door flew open.

"Get out on the wall, now!" Mr. Brown yelled. "And, don't act like you two don't know what's going on!" Smiley and I did our best imitation of two sleepy, confused fish as we emerged from our hole rubbing the sleep from our eyes. The other freshmen were performing similar acts as they were being driven out into the hall by the sophomores.

We could all hear the pounding from Mr. Ingram still trapped within his room. The pissheads were scurrying up and down the hallway, frantically trying to determine who had been hit. It seems Mr. Coffman, Mr. Ingram's roommate, had called one of them on the phone and alerted them as to what had happened. Knowing only a junior or senior could remove the stick from the door, they could only wait and hope Mr.Ingram could shake it loose from within. After all, their only hope for revenge rested with Ingram since he was the only one who could guess who had participated.

Suddenly, it happened. The stick slipped from the doorknob and fell to the floor with an eerie thud. The feeling of sheer terror swept over me as my legs began to shake.

"Stay calm," I kept telling myself. "He'll never suspect you were in on it."

My life seemed to flash before my eyes as Mr. Ingram stepped from his room. A pall of subdued terror hung in the hall as he made his way toward us.

"Why did I join the Corps?" I again wondered as Mr. Ingram approached.

"Someone's dead!" he said in a tone of voice that let each of us know he was serious. Mr. Ingram took pride in his discipline, and we knew this would be a major blow to his ego.

"Go ahead and take your three picks," Mr. London said as all of the juniors and seniors watched in amusement. "You know the rules. If you get all three guesses right, the whole class is yours until first call."

The tension could have been cut with a knife as Mr. Ingram and the rest of the sophomore class looked over us, one by one. I tried to keep my legs from shaking, but found it impossible. Mr. Ingram moved from freshman to freshman, placing his fist over each heart. By detecting the intensity of our heart beats, he could better guess which ones might have been directly involved.

"Smiley," Mr. Ingram said with a tone of confidence.

"One for one," Mr. London responded. My heart began to race.

"Maybe one of the sophomores saw us," I wondered. "No, they couldn't have," I rationalized. "Smiley and I were in our hole before anyone could have seen us."

"Adair," Mr. Ingram chose next.

"Two for two," Mr.London replied.

"That's it. I'm finished," I silently concluded. I was too new to be directly involved in something like this. I really hadn't yet proven my ability to perform. The Pissheads would never let me forget it if I were selected next — and neither would the other freshmen.

"Go start the steam showers," Mr. Ingram told another sophomore as he walked toward me. My heart was now beating with such fervor that I could actually feel my entire chest pulsating.

Mr. Ingram stopped in front of me, looked me in the eye and pressed his fist into my chest. After what seemed like an eternity, he leaned over and, with a pert tightening of his lips whispered, "Fish Quinn, so help me, if you had anything to do with this, you're dead." Anything I would have said would have been a mistake, so I remained silent.

Suddenly, from down the hall one of the other sophomores hollered, "I think fish Roosma was the other one in on it. I saw him scrambling to his hole right after it happened, and he's got water all over his shorts."

Mr. Ingram's eyes, like dark holes in a mask, fastened on me. From the silence I could hear the ticks of a clock coming from a room behind the wall where I stood. He walked down the hall and placed his fist on Roosma's chest, comparing the speed of his heartbeat with mine. He quickly returned to feel mine again and, after what seemed like an eternity, he said, "Roosma."

My heart skipped a beat as the weight of a thousand pounds ascended from my shoulders.

"Nope," Mr. London said. "You've got Smiley and Adair for two hours. The rest of you fish hit the bag."

With the atmosphere in the hall still morbidly tense, Mr. Ingram watched me turn and walk back toward my hole.

"I hope you weren't stupid enough to be involved in this, Quinn," he said as I walked past him.

"No, sir," I responded with an oscar-winning voice.

As I approached my hole, I could feel his cold stare focusing on the back of my neck. According to the rules, the sophomores were never supposed to find out who was involved once the choices had been made. Unfortunately, the dreaded grapevine had its own way of allowing classified information to somehow leak out. I knew they would eventually find out.

"Smiley and Adair, you two have 60 seconds to be back out here in your sweats and combat boots. Move!" Mr. Ingram commanded.

Smiley quickly entered our hole and began to change for the crap out.

"What do you think he's going to do with you guys?" I asked as he frantically laced up his combat boots.

"Hear that water running?" he said. "Does that answer your question? It's steam shower time. Oh, well. I couldn't sleep anyway."

He was right. I could hear the steam showers running from the end of the hall.

"You sure are lucky, Quinn," he said as he stepped from the room.

I shut the door, turned off the lights, and climbed into bed knowing there was no logical reason why I hadn't also been caught. Were it not for the Roosma's idea — putting water on his shorts as a decoy, I probably would have been chosen. We all knew the risk involved and agreed that we would fulfil our mission, each taking the chance of getting crapped out if caught.

I had indeed been lucky this time and couldn't help reliving what had just occurred, over and over in my mind as I listened to the echo of Adair and Smiley counting as they pushed amidst the sound of running water.

Again, I questioned my decision to enter the Corps and wondered how all of this could possibly benefit me in the future.

"Why am I putting up with all of this?" I asked myself as my eyes began to feel heavy. I continued to push the thought of quitting from my mind and soon found myself unable to concentrate. Only now did I feel the fatigue slowly flooding my entire body. As the sound of the steam showers faded, I gently slipped from consciousness and fell into a deep sleep.

CHAPTER 7

A FRESHMAN'S PRIVILEGE

Aloud whistle blasted from just outside the door, jolting me from my sleep. It was fish Probst with the first call for morning chow. The door opened as I slid from my bunk. Fish Smiley staggered in, soaking wet from head to toe, most of it sweat.

"I'm dead," he said as he flopped onto his bed and closed his eyes, hoping to get a few seconds of rest.

"You look dead," I replied, not really knowing what else to say.

"That's the last douche out I'm helping with," he moaned as he tried to force himself back to an upright position. He slowly rose from the bed as a rider, thrown from his horse, remounts to overcome his shock.

"Mr. Ingram's really pissed about all of this," he said.

"We all figured he would be. That's part of the reason we did it." I said.

"He pretty much figures you were the other one, but we wouldn't tell him."

"Thanks. I really appreciate that. I'm sure he'll find out soon enough, and I'll get mine before it's all said and done."

We prepared for morning inspection knowing the sophomores would be looking especially hard for any reason to make us push. We were right. Though no grudges were supposed to be held, they found plenty of reasons to put us on our face that morning. Actually, we sort of enjoyed it, knowing we had made our point the previous night.

They knew now that we could hold our own. Once an incident like this occurs, the sophomores realize they, too, are vulnerable. No one especially relishes the thought of being awakened by a cold bucket of water in the face while sound asleep.

As the day passed and time progressed, things pretty much returned to normal, though I did hear sly remarks from time to time from the sophomore class about my possible participation in the late night excursion. I continued my study of campusology questions, amidst my required course work and within a couple of months had gradually gained full acceptance within the freshman class of Squadron Two. As my confidence increased, so did my inquisitiveness. I began to test the limits placed on us as fish. I eventually figured it was I who was paying for the education and wanted to have some fun, or at least see how much I could get away with. I knew I would have to be extremely careful, not wanting the rest of the fish to get crapped out for trying something on my own.

One risky stunt occurred during C.Q. when Smiley and I scared the living tar out of fish Roosma and fish Probst. I had decided to climb out of our window and light a couple of firecrackers on their window sill while they studied. Our windows were normally kept open during C.Q., and I knew that if I could get back into our hole without getting caught, there would be no way for the upperclassmen to prove who had done it.

With Smiley keeping watch, I quickly crawled out of our window and quietly made my way to Probst and Roosma's hole. I was forced to sneak across the grass in order to get to their hole, crouching as I passed beneath several upperclassmen's windows. Walking on the grass was a senior privilege, so I knew I needed to get back as quickly as possible. A freshman caught on the grass without a senior's permission was as good as dead.

I reached their window and slowly peeked over the ledge. They were both studying at their desks, just inches inside. I carefully lit the firecrackers, sat them inside the window sill, then scampered back to my hole. Just as I leaped back through our window, stumbling across Smiley's desk, two explosions occurred. Screams echoed across the quad from Probst and Roosma's hole. Within seconds, the hallway was filled with upperclassmen trying to figure out what had just occurred.

Smiley and I grappled to clean up the mess I had made and tried to regain our composure, knowing someone would soon be looking for the culprits. We could hear Probst and Roosma pleading their innocence to the upperclassmen as they were interrogated by Mr. Lane and the rest of the senior class. Mr. London had already begun to survey the hall hoping to uncover some obvious clues. The smell of gunpowder was evident as he opened our door and stuck his head inside.

"You guys seen anybody outside tonight?" he asked suspiciously.

"No, sir," we chorused without hesitation.

"Mr. London, sir. Fish Quinn requests permission to make a statement, sir."

"What," he answered.

"It's not a fish privilege to look out of our window, sir."

"Probst and Roosma are saying someone threw a couple of firecrackers into their hole a few minutes ago while they were studying; almost killed 'em. Burned a hole right through Roosma's psychology book. Their ears are still ringing. You two know who may have done it?"

"No, sir," we answered again.

"Steam shower privileges this weekend if you tell me."

A brief silence fell upon us. I couldn't afford to let fish Smiley think about it too long.

"No, sir," I said.

"If I find out you guys are lying, you've had it," he threatened.

Shutting the door he hesitated, throwing me a quick inquisitive glance, hoping to detect a smile. With no response, he closed the door. As far as we were concerned, it was a freshman's privilege to deny guilt and an upperclassman's job to prove it. "Boy, steam shower privileges would have been nice," Smiley jokingly sneered. I simply smiled, knowing we had been successful.

A small war soon erupted between Roosma, Probst, Smiley and I, once they found out we had accomplished the dirty deed. We tried our best to get each other in trouble without putting the rest of the freshman class at risk. This became extremely difficult at times, knowing the sophomores would devour any opportunity to prove disharmony among members of our class.

One afternoon while Probst and Roosma were showering, I snuck into their hole and removed Probst's name tag from his uniform. I returned it to it's proper position — only upside down. Since they were always in a hurry to get dressed, Probst didn't notice it and fell out for evening inspection completely unaware of what was about to happen. I waited in suspense as Mr. Reed began to inspect him.

"Is this some sort of joke, Probst?" he suddenly belted out.

A look of confusion appeared on fish Probst's face as he stood erect up against the wall trying to figure out what Mr. Reese was talking about. A group of sophomores quickly gathered in front of Probst, laughing harshly as they pointed at his name tag. After a brief discussion the sophomores decided to make fish Roosma do push ups for not inspecting Probst's uniform prior to inspection.

"Why is your name tag on upside down, fish Probst?" Mr. Reed asked, scowling. Probst continued to look perplexed, as if he somehow wanted to justify the error that had mysteriously occurred, but he didn't know how to formulate his rational. I avoided direct eye contact with him as his old lady began to push. I knew he was looking in my direction hoping to elicit some sort of response. "Sir, fish Probst requests permission to make a statement, sir!" he finally said.

"Go ahead," Mr. Reed answered, "but don't piss on my leg!"

After a moment of consideration, Probst began, "Sir, not being informed to the highest degree of accuracy, I hesitate to articulate for fear that I may deviate from the true course of rectitude. In short, sir I am a very dumb fish and do not know, sir!"

"Sir, not being informed ..." Mr, Reed mimicked savagely in a high pitched, squirmy sort-of voice.

After a class set of push ups Roosma was required to fix Probst's name tag, then shout, "Thank you, fish bud!" from only inches from Probst's face.

As the semester proceeded, rumor of our on-going battle somehow leaked to the upperclassmen, making it increasingly difficult to evade persecution from the pissheads. They knew what was going on, but could do nothing without evidence. I have to admit, we took a certain amount of pleasure in their frustration. It became a cat and mouse game; we pulled things out, and they tried to catch us. They began to threaten some of the other fish, claiming we were destroying the class unity. We disagreed and, though we had several close calls, we were never blatantly caught. It was simply our way of relieving some of the day to day pressure.

Another exciting moment occurred for me later my freshman year when I was randomly selected to become an Officer of the Day for the upcoming "Elephant Bowl." The Elephant Bowl is a charity event that consists of a full contact football game between senior Corps members.

Air Force seniors join with the seniors in the Aggie Band to challenge those of the Army, Navy and Marine units. Each team practices for one month in preparation for the game and is coached by a volunteer varsity football player.

The annual event takes place on a Saturday afternoon at Kyle Field. As one of the Officers of the Day, I would be allowed to stand on the sidelines and symbolically guard the field from intruders during the game. During actual Aggie football games, seniors from each outfit are selected as Officers of the Day and are to stand on the side lines, sabres and all, to act as symbolic guardians. It was my opportunity to get a small taste of what being a zip felt like.

I was allowed to dress in full senior attire, except for the senior riding boots. The only time we were even allowed to touch senior boots was when we pulled them from a senior's foot, which we were often called upon to do. The outfit rounded up numerous ribbons and medals from several cadets and pinned them to the front of my shirt. The most exciting part of the event was the opportunity I had to carry a sabre, which was normally reserved for those in Corps leadership positions. It was almost too much excitement for a freshman frog to handle.

Five fish yell leaders were also randomly selected for the game. They purchased overalls, similar to those worn by the actual yell leaders, and were expected to learn the various moves in preparation for leading yells for those in attendance.

The Elephant Bowl had traditionally been dominated by the Army, Navy, and Marine team, and this year was no exception. The Air Force team was crushed, meaning we would probably be the brunt of jokes for the next several weeks.

"Just wait until we become seniors," fish Garrett commented after the game. "We're going to kick some tail if I have anything to say about it. You plan on playing, Quinn?" he asked as we left the stadium to return to the quad.

"Wouldn't miss it for the world," I answered. "If I survive that long."

"Keep messing around with Roosma and Probst," he said, "and you probably won't."

CHAPTER 8

GUIDE-ON BEARER

My proficiency in uniform preparation slowly, but surely, improved as I became more accustomed to the expectations of the pissheads. Smiley taught me how to achieve a superior shine on my shoes by using a cotton cloth, black shoe polish, and a little bit of good old fashioned spit. By tightly wrapping a 100% cotton t-shirt around my right index finger, I was able to achieve a glass like reflection on my shoes, more commonly known as a "spit shine."

The brass insignia worn on our uniform was polished prior to both morning and evening inspection. No marks or scratches were allowed on any brass, including name tags and belt buckles. Each piece of brass had its proper location on the uniform and was expected to be within a fraction of the accepted tolerance at all times. The pissheads often appeared with a ruler during inspections to insure everything was exact.

Rule after rule, procedure after procedure was drilled into my head until each became instinctive. We were required to know, by name, each upperclassmen in our four story dorm. We were also expected to remember each upperclassman we met on a daily basis. It was not uncommon to meet well over 20 upperclassmen in one day. The more names a fish could remember, the sharper he appeared to the upperclassmen — which meant potential positions of authority and increased responsibility.

I decided to pursue my goal of becoming guide-on bearer and knew a competition would soon be held for those interested in holding the position. The guide-on bearer is primarily responsible for maintaining the outfit flag and must carry it alongside the commanding officer during all marching exhibitions. During outfit runs, the guide-on bearer carries the flag high above his head with both hands. The guide-on is never allowed to drop below shoulder height at any time while running.

I informed Mr. Tevis, the current guide-on bearer, of my interest in the position and scheduled practices with him whenever time permitted. During these practices, Mr. Tevis taught me the various maneuvers that would be required during formations and marching competitions. I borrowed the guide-on numerous times and practiced each maneuver until I had them perfected.

The guide-on competition was preceded by the "Sharpest Fish" competition, which is conducted solely by the junior class. I felt my chances of being selected as guide-on bearer would increase dramatically if I could do well in the first competition, which was devised to select the sharpest fish in the outfit.

No one really knew how to prepare for the sharpest fish competition because the details were kept secret. All we knew was the uniform requirement; long sleeve shirt, white gloves and ascot. During this competition I came to the conclusion that the ascot was the only piece of the Aggie uniform that was more uncomfortable than boot straps and, because of this, could only be worn for short periods of time.

The ascot consisted of a single piece of material that snapped around the neck, then pulled down the front of the chest under the shirt. I don't know who devised this piece of uniform, or why, but concluded they must have had a great sense of humor. We were taught the tighter the ascot appeared, the sharper the freshman looked.

In order to obtain a drum tight appearance, we pinned the ascot underneath our uniform to both our underwear and t-shirt. This pulled the ascot in several directions allowing it to remain tight and wrinkle free. Only Aggies know this secret, and I don't think anybody else would even care to attempt it. A good tight ascot has a tendency to cut off the circulation in the neck and shoulders if not properly prepared.

Very few people outside of the Corps understand the torture a freshman or sophomore goes through during football games or marching competitions when the ascot is required. After putting it on for the first time, I understood why the juniors and seniors opted to wear ties instead.

As I prepared for my interview with the juniors, I pinned the ascot to the front of my underwear and to several locations on my t-shirt. I'm not sure why it mattered if my ascot looked tight or not, but concluded that if it helped the upperclassmen separate the sharp cadets from the mediocre cadets, it just might increase my chances of acquiring the guide-on bearer position. I made up my mind to simply suffer for a few minutes, hoping the eventual results would be worth it.

As I finalized my uniform preparation, the ascot slowly began to pull my underwear up in the front, causing it to eventually reach beyond the middle of my stomach, not to mention what was happening in the back. I figured my only relief was a good sense of humor, since there was nothing else I could do about it anyway.

I walked down the hall and knocked three times on Mr. London's door, not really knowing what to expect.

"Come in, fish Quinn!" he yelled.

I opened the door and stepped inside. The room was filled with juniors, each one staring at me in silence. I knew I was expected to greet each one, beginning with Mr. London, since he was in charge.

"Howdy Mr. London, sir!" I began.

Every junior in the room then began to speak simultaneously, wanting me to greet them next. As I attempted to speak to each one in turn, I was interrupted and chastised for omitting someone. It was like trying to listen to fifteen radio stations broadcasting at the same time on the same frequency. I soon realized they were testing my nerves and were attempting to get me frustrated, hoping I would lose my composure. Amidst the confusion, I cleared my head and continued to speak to each junior in descending order of rank. Though they couldn't hear me through the noise, I continued anyway.

After finally greeting each junior, I began to answer questions. Again, each junior was asking questions simultaneously, so I attempted to complete one before beginning another. During each of my responses, an attempt was made to divert my attention to another individual's question. This fiasco continued for about five minutes. Suddenly, the room fell silent.

"Have a seat, fish Quinn," Mr. London said, pointing to an empty chair in the middle of the room. As I did so, I noticed each of the juniors visually inspecting my uniform in an attempt to find something out of place.

"Fish Quinn," Mr. London began. "did you know your name tag is upside down?" My heart skipped a beat as my mind instantly flashed back to each phase of my uniform preparation.

"Could Probst or Roosma have done this to me?" I thought. "They couldn't have," I rationalized. "I checked everything over twice!" Within a second or two, I came to the conclusion that Mr. London was simply testing my confidence and was hoping I would glance down to look at my name tag. I looked him in the eye and said, "Sir, my uniform is perfect."

"Are you sure your ribbons are in the correct order?" Mr. Steel asked.

"Yes, sir," I responded with confidence.

"Just checking," he said with a slight grin.

They proceeded to quiz me on my campusology proficiency. I answered each without flaw. Next came the current event questions. I felt confident about my responses. Mr. London then asked me what position I aspired to the following year.

"Guide-on Bearer, sir," I answered without hesitation.

"If you become guide-on bearer, that means you'll have to walk out front with me. What makes you think I want you to walk next to me?" he asked.

"Sir," I began, "Fish Quinn requests permission to make a statement, sir."

"What?"

"It's not a fish privilege to think, sir."

"Very good, fish Quinn. Let me rephrase the question. What makes you contemplate I would want you next to me with the guide-on?"

Knowing I could not say the word "want," I quickly replaced it with "desire."

"Because I desire it more than any other fish in the outfit, sir."

They chuckled, but realized I had gained much confidence since I had frogged in just a few short months earlier.

"Well, good luck to you," Mr. London said. "I hope you get it. You're free to go now."

I rose to attention, did a quick about-face and walked to the door. There, I performed another about-face and said, "Mr. London, sir, fish Quinn requests permission to ask a question, sir."

"Go ahead," Mr. London responded.

"Fish Quinn requests permission to take off, sir."

"Permission granted, fish Quinn," he answered.

I performed one more precise turn and exited the room. With a silent sigh of relief I shut the door behind me.

"I wonder if I appeared over confident?" I thought to myself as I walked down the hall to my hole. "Oh well, I've got nothing to lose," I concluded as I entered my hole.

Several freshmen had gathered awaiting to hear what had happened. I was, however, unable to give them any advice, as I had given my Aggie word of honor to the juniors I would not reveal any information concerning what had just occurred. Nothing is more sacred to an Aggie than his word of honor. We were taught that Aggies do not lie, cheat, or steal, and we were not to tolerate anyone that did.

Fish Smiley eventually won the Sharpest Fish Competition, and he deserved it. He had been involved in several key activities, which had given him exposure and recognition among other members of the Corps. He took the Corps much more seriously than most of the other freshmen and aspired to be the outfit commander one day. I felt much of his Corps perspective came from his membership in the Fish Drill Team, where the daily pressure on him was tremendous.

Each afternoon, Smiley would meticulously prepare his stiffly starched fatigue uniform for Fish Drill Team practice, while keeping a close eye on the drill rifle he was responsible for. He kept this drill rifle locked to a water pipe in our hole and protected it with his life. Should a member of the Fish Drill Team ever lose his rifle, amen to that fish.

His hair was kept very short. As a matter of fact, he was almost bald, especially prior to drill competitions. On several occasions I used his razor to shave any excess hair from his neck in order to avoid point deductions during these competitions.

By now I had became somewhat accustomed to the rigid lifestyle within the Corps and actually began to enjoy many aspects of it. I enjoyed sports and found it an outlet and an opportunity to become an integral part of the fish class. I won "All University" honors in the intra-mural wrestling competition, adding points to our quest for the fish sports flag. Victory for me was sweet, as I managed to pin a pisshead in the Corps during the third period of the final match.

I began to feel equal to the other fish and continued to look for opportunities to pull out special privileges normally reserved for upper-classmen. As long as I was careful and covered my tracks, I knew they couldn't do anything to me. The sophomores knew this, too, and it frustrated them. Though they had ways of applying their own pressure, they could not accuse any fish of misconduct unless caught.

The sophomores would often attempt to fracture our class unity by threats of punishment for us allowing our own fish buds to break the rules. One of the ways they frustrated us was through our "fish matches." As freshmen, we were to keep a box of matches with us at all times. Each box contained 30 wooden matches. We were required to write our name and squadron number on the alternating four sides of each match. This was a meticulous and time consuming task and none of us looked forward to repeating it.

Periodically, the pissheads would inspect our fish matches, hoping one of us had forgotten our box or didn't have the correct number of matches. Whenever a discrepancy occurred, the pissheads would collect each box and burn them. They then would require each of us to prepare a new box prior to the next scheduled inspection. Again, peer pressure became the key to each freshman conforming to requirements, eventually uniting us as a team.

We were continuously warned not to allow anyone within our ranks to break the rules. For the most part, we held together and maintained our silence. It became a constant struggle within our class to try to have some fun without getting the rest of the fish class in too much trouble. Some just wanted to be left alone and were simply trying to survive the year, while others looked for every opportunity to frustrate the pissheads. I happened to be one of the "others."

I just couldn't let the sophomores run all over us without getting a little bit of revenge. Whenever we wanted to get them off our backs, we simply circulated the rumor of a potential douche out that night. This would normally cause them to lose a few hours of sleep, wondering if there were any truth to the rumor. In addition to all of the Corps requirements, there was also the constant pressure to maintain a decent grade-point average, in order to avoid scholastic probation. Many cadets, unfortunately, gave the Corps priority over school assignments and did not return due to poor grades. The ability to balance Corps activities and school assignments was incredibly difficult.

We each eventually devised our own ways of relieving stress from the day to day pressures faced as a fish. Fish Jumper and I would often secretly simulate the unique Ross Volunteer march, in the hall, knowing full well we would pay a severe price if caught. The Ross Volunteers are a select group of junior and senior cadets chosen each year to become the national honor guards for the Governor of Texas.

They are also responsible for the monthly 21-gun salute ceremony held on campus called "Silver Taps." This ceremony is performed each month in honor of Aggies who have recently passed away. They wore white uniforms during their official assignments, which posed a particular problem for fish. We were never allowed to acknowledge their existence when they wore these white uniforms. Behind closed doors we called them "ghosts." On several occasions Mr. London and Mr. Calvert would speak to us while dressed in white, hoping we would respond. We simply acted like they didn't exist, trying not to give them any reason for disciplinary action.

One evening per month, we extinguished all lights on campus and silently walked to the Academic building where Silver Taps took place. It was always an amazing experience to see thousands of students walk across the dark campus without a word being spoken. As the students surrounded the area, the Ross Volunteers would slowly march to the center of the area to perform a 21-gun salute for the fallen Aggies. After the shots had been fired, several cadets with trumpets played Silver Taps from high atop the Academic building.

Following the ceremony, we would, again, silently return to our dorms where all lights were required to remain extinguished for the remainder of the evening. Silver Taps constantly reminds all Aggies that mortality is temporary, and one day it will be performed for each of us. It is not only performed in honor of our fallen comrades but also their families, who were often in attendance.

Marching became second nature to us during the year. Almost every afternoon we gathered as a fish class outside of the dorm in white t-shirt, blue jeans, and military shoes to prepare for our daily drill practice. Day after day, we marched and perfected our maneuvers to the commands of an upperclassman in preparation for the fish drill competition. During this freshman marching competition, each fish was expected to lead the rest of the class through various formations and maneuvers.

Day after day, fish Smiley and I rehearsed commands and movements in the cramped confines of our hole, hoping to become proficient enough to keep the formation from getting tangled up during the competition. It was finally after winning the Best Drilled Freshman award that I actually felt I had a chance of becoming the next guide-on bearer for Squadron Two.

By this time, those of us that remained realized that we actually might make it to see Final Review. It was now time for each of us to compete for the sophomore position we wanted. Out of the four cadets that had frogged into Squadron Two that year, I was the only one that remained. For me, guide-on bearer was all that mattered now. The competition for the position would include several phases; guide-on proficiency, uniform inspection, campusology proficiency, and overall military bearing.

Mr. Tevis, the current guide-on bearer, was responsible for conducting the competition and would have the final say as to who would hold the position the following year.

Smiley assisted as I prepared my uniform for my turn. I was the last of six candidates and wanted to look my best, knowing Mr. Tevis felt appearance was paramount. Ascots and white gloves again were required, which made the guide-on maneuvers more difficult. The gloves were slippery and the ascots were, as mentioned previously, very uncomfortable.

I felt I did well during the inspection and knew I was in the running as the competition drew to a close. I nervously awaited the results as the sophomore class met to approve the winner.

Tevis entered my hole on a warm spring afternoon. Extending his hand, he said, "Congratulations, fish Quinn. You'll be the next guide-on bearer for Gator Two, assuming you make it through the next hour. You've got five minutes to get dressed and be outside in white shirt, blue jeans, and military shoes. I'll be waiting for you outside with the guide-on."

"Yes, sir!" I responded, barely able to contain my excitement. "Congratulations, Quinn," Smiley said as Mr. Tevis shut the door. "I wonder what he has in store for you?"

"What do you mean?" I asked.

"Probably some sort of initiation. You always knew you would get yours. Looks like today's the day."

I dressed quickly, slightly worried about what I was about to experience, but the excitement of the moment seemed to alleviate most of my nervousness. As I left my hole, I remembered the time Smiley had stumbled in after his early morning crap out.

"Surely they wouldn't put me through something like that for doing something good?" I thought. Once again, I was wrong.

I was outside in exactly three minutes flat, ready for whatever Mr. Tevis had in store for me.

"This belongs to your class now," he said as he handed the guide-on to me. "Protect it with your life."

"Yes, sir," I replied.

"Wait a minute," he said as he quickly snatched it back from me. "Why don't you drop and give me a class set first?"

I immediately dropped and performed a class set of push ups. As I counted off the last push up, he ordered me back to attention. I took the guide-on and again came to attention. He informed me of my obligation during outfit runs.

"Do you think you can carry the guide-on above your head for a few miles?" he asked.

"Mr Tevis, sir," I began. "Fish Quinn requests permission to make a statement, sir."

"What is it?"

"It's not a fish privilege to think, sir."

"Very good," he replied. "Let's go."

I followed, carrying the guide-on at my right side, while he began to march. "This isn't going to be so bad," I thought.

"Double time, march!" he yelled.

We broke into a trot. I lifted the guide-on high above my head and somehow sensed other eyes upon us. We circled the quad, running past several dorms. I could hear supportive cheers from the windows above.

"Whoop! Good bull!" someone hollered.

"Looking good, Quinn!" someone else yelled from the vicinity of our dorm.

My adrenaline began to pump as we picked up the pace. With arms raised, I held the guide-on high above my head as if to say "Hey, look at me! I'm an Aggie, and I'm a member of the Corps of Cadets!." The pride and spirit swelled within me as Mr. Tevis jodied and I echoed his words. I knew that I could now do whatever Mr. Tevis required.

After two trips around the quad, Mr. Tevis veered across the street and headed toward the golf course near the main entrance of the campus. "Oh, no," I thought. "Where is he taking me?"

We reached the northwest corner of the golf course when Mr. Tevis gave me the command to stop.

"I'll hold the guide-on," he began, "while you give me another class set of push ups." I handed him the guide-on, dropped and began to push.

"One, sir! Two, sir! Three, sir!" I counted as I pushed. At the conclusion of eighty-one push ups, I requested permission to get up. Permission was granted and again we began to run, this time to the main entrance of campus.

We reached the northeast corner of the golf course and I was again ordered to perform a class set of push ups. My arms were becoming weak, but I managed to complete the class set again. "Let's go!" he commanded as I rose from the grass.

Again, I lifted the guide-on above my head and followed as we ran to the southeast corner of campus. By now my arms were becoming numb, yet I was determined not to give up. My arms began to droop as I attempted to keep the guide-on above my head. I was again told to do eighty-one push ups as we reached the southeast corner of campus. Several student golfers watched as I attempted another class set.

By now Mr. Tevis could see I was exhausted, and he wasn't quite as picky about my posture. All I could do was shake my head as I counted and hope he knew how I felt. As I rose from my futile attempt to complete the push ups, Mr. Tevis told me to take a couple of deep breaths.

"This is the last stretch," he said. I was relieved to hear this, but I knew it wasn't over yet. We ran toward the decending sun and reached the south-west corner of the golf course.

"Last time," he said looking to gauge the effect of his remark. I handed him the guide-on with a slight hesitation.

"After this set you'll be the new guide-on bearer for Gator Two."

By this point I could not even hold myself up. He grabbed the back of my belt and lifted me off the ground.

"I'll give you a hand with this set," he said. "I had the same problem last year during my initiation." He pulled me off the ground each time I counted. I'm sure those passing by wondered what was going on as he stood over me, lifting with each attempted push.

Upon reaching eighty-one I said, "Mr. Tevis, sir, fish Quinn requests permission to ask a question, sir!"

"Yes?" he answered a bit sarcastically.

"Fish Quinn requests permission to get up, sir!"

"Permission granted and congratulations," he said as he handed me the guide-on. "You're now the guide-on bearer for Squadron Two. Ready for the run back?" he asked, knowing I could not do another push up.

"Yes, sir," I replied.

"What did you say? I couldn't hear you."

"Yes, sir!" I said for all within shouting distance to hear.

"Good," he replied. "And look sharp. There's probably going to be a few people watching when we get back to the quad, and I don't want you to embarrass me."

As we began the short run back, I felt what a marathon runner must experience as he enters the stadium after a long and grueling run. Though no cheers were heard, never had I felt a sense of accomplishment like this before. I had been pushed this day far beyond what I had ever imagined possible and, the amazing thing about it, was that I felt good about it.

"This is what's it's all about," I surmised as we ran back to the quad, guide-on held high. "This is what creates the spirit I saw in those cadets at midnight yell practice last year."

Realizing the potential in each of us and going far beyond what we had limited ourselves to — in this case, physically — is what creates the motivation and desire to achieve even more. I realized I was no longer at Texas A&M simply to receive an education; I could get that anywhere. Only in the Corps of Cadets could I develop the leadership qualities I would need to one day overcome seemingly impossible obstacles. I was learning to endure. I was learning commitment, the kind of commitment that would one day assist me in other areas of my life. I knew now that there was no way that I could ever quit.

As we circled the quad, I was exhausted, out of breath and my arms ached, but, somehow, I felt as if I could go on and on. Though my body was telling me differently, I knew it was worth it. I finally understood what was happening. Only now did I know what it meant to be a member of the Corps of Cadets. Most of all, I knew what it meant to be an Aggie!

CHAPTER 9

WHAT DOES YOUR MOTHER CALL YOU?

Sparkey's was packed the night I made guide-on bearer. I celebrated with my Gator fish buds to the country tunes of "Silver Wings" and "Pop a Top Again" on the old cement floor. Sparkey's was a small hang-out across the street from the main entrance to Texas A&M. In the back room there was a small cement dance floor surrounded by a black wall covered with florescent graffiti that had been painted throughout the years by various cadets in the Corps.

On rainy nights the roof would leak, so we would place buckets at various locations on the dance floor to catch the dripping water. With a little bit of practice, we were able to two-step around each bucket as we danced to the music from an old jukebox that must have been at least 20 years old. The needle in the jukebox was worn and often skipped at random across several of the old records as they played.

It was here that I became fairly proficient at the Texas Two-Step, Cotton Eyed Joe, Waltz, Polka and Shottish. These were the same dances my parents and grandparents had learned in their younger days and still enjoyed.

Going to Sparkey's was like stepping back into time. There, our day to day challenges seemed to fade with the music and laughter that went on well into the night. Every cadet at A&M was expected to be able to slide across a saw dust floor at the drop of a hat, and the girls were not expected to wait around for an invitation. Thanks to Lisa Day, a friend I made during the semester, I was fairly proficient at the various steps. I credit her with my ability to actually turn 360 degrees while doing the two step, without stomping on my partner's toes in the process. Each Wednesday night we would gather at a larger dance hall called Lakeview, just outside of Bryan. Thursday was student night and admission was free. I took advantage of every opportunity to save what little money I had. The wooden dance floor was large enough to accommodate several hundred people, and everyone danced in a counter clock wise motion, decreasing the possibility of collision.

These evenings played an important role in our ability to cope as freshmen within the Corps. An outlet from the rigid military lifestyle was periodically needed. Sparkey's and Lakeview provided this outlet for us.

At Texas A&M, we had the best of both worlds: that of the camaraderie the Corps provided, along with the periodic ability to escape and associate with coeds and other students outside the Corps environment. Unlike other military institutions, we were encouraged to maintain friendships outside the Corps and could acquire permission periodically to leave the campus. This gave us much needed relief and helped us avoid the "burn out" syndrome that often occurs within other military institutions. With only 3,000 of the 30,000 students at Texas A&M enrolled in the Corps, there was ample opportunity to acquire numerous friends outside our military surroundings through the various activities and associations at the university.

Other than specific weekends, a "free night out" had to be earned by fish in the Corps. This privilege could be acquired for numerous reasons: excellent grades, outstanding performance, or for other special occasions. Free nights out were extremely effective motivational tools used by the upperclassmen in their attempt to teach us obedience. Unfortunately, the opposite was also true. If a fish received too many gigs, or rams, weekend privileges were eliminated.

As our final exams approached, we all sensed the beginning of the end. It became extremely difficult for the sophomores to enforce our strict adherence to the rules, though they insisted we remain a unified class prior to our final crap out. Elephant Walk became the symbolic event that led us to believe for the first time we would soon become pisheads. Elephant Walk is a tradition that signifies the end of the seniors' reign and, for the cadets, the opportunity for the juniors to assume control of the Corps. This is also the juniors' first opportunity to acknowledge the words "zip" and "elephant," both representative of a senior at A&M.

The entire senior class, both male and female, Corps and non-Corps, paraded around campus signifying old elephants about to die. As they did so, the juniors hid in strategic locations around the campus and simulated wild game hunters. Some juniors went as far as to secure jeeps and armored vehicles from a local guard unit to create additional realism. An eventual wrestling match ensued in each outfit between the juniors and seniors when they finally returned to the quad.

Of course we, as fish, were not allowed to watch any of this occur. Smiley and I secretly peered from behind closed blinds, watching it all, hoping no one would catch us. Later that evening, the two classes gathered off campus to celebrate and reflect upon the friendships made and the growth that had occurred during their three year association in the Corps.

Elephant Walk also meant that we would soon have our first "drop handle" crap out, beginning first with the seniors. Drop handle crap outs were designed to give fish the opportunity to earn the right to finally address the upperclassmen by their first names. It was one of the final steps in being accepted as a unified class by the upperclassmen. It also gave the upperclassmen the opportunity to test our endurance one last time.

During the week following Elephant Walk, rumors began to surface that the seniors had set a date for our drop- handle crap out. I nervously wondered just what would actually happen to us. I had heard horror stories about drop handle crap outs and was unsure about what to expect. I figured we would have to pay a dear price before the seniors would allow us to address them by their first names.

Finally, the official word came on a Thursday afternoon. Mr. Lane entered our hole as Smiley and I were preparing for evening chow. "Tomorrow," he began. "Five o'clock. Fatigue uniform with outfit hats. Don't be late. Any questions?"

"No, sir!" we responded in unison.

As he shut the door, Smiley and I stood there in amazement, not knowing what to say. Finally, Smiley held out his hand and said "Congratulations, pisshead. Looks like we made it."

I found it extremely difficult to concentrate in any of my classes the following day. I just couldn't believe that, by evening chow, I would be calling the seniors by their first names, that is, if I survived the crap out.

Five o'clock finally arrived and, as we filed out into the hall, we realized this would be no cake walk. The seniors were already yelling at the top of their lungs. They apparently wanted to show the sophomores how it was done, or at least how they used to do it. Before we knew it, we had performed a class set and were outside, running toward a near-by park for a little lesson in old fashioned calisthenics.

We saw this as an opportunity to prove to the senior class we were indeed united. Each of us had made a commitment not to quit, no matter what. Spirits were high. We now worked together like a fine-tuned machine, assisting each other as needed.

After several more push-up sessions, we were told to simulate an air attack. We ran, then dove for cover each time a senior yelled "hit it!" We were then directed to crawl down a small stream running through campus, making careful our heads were not exposed to the invisible bullets zipping overhead from the imaginary enemy planes.

While still soaking wet, we followed behind the seniors to Kyle Field. Once inside the stadium, we ran from sideline to sideline, across the hot, humid artificial turf as the seniors continued to yell. With the heat and humidity intense, I began to feel a little light headed. After several wind sprints, I soon realized I could no longer contain the nauseating feeling that had overcome me and quickly ran to the nearest side line drain. There I was joined by several other freshmen with the same problem. Together, we relieved ourselves, much to the amusement of the senior class.

We finally concluded our wind sprints and headed out of the stadium and off campus to an unfamiliar location. Eventually, we were told to stop and line up against a fence that bordered an old dirt road. The seniors formed a line behind Mr. Lane and began to shake our hands.

"Fish Quinn," Mr. Lane said as he reached me, hand extended. "What does your mother call you?"

"Dan," I replied.

"My mother calls me Dale," he said. "It's nice to meet you, Dan."

"It's nice to meet you, Dale," I said with a huge grin and a sigh of relief, knowing the hard part was finally over.

One by one, each senior dropped handles with us and formally ended their leadership role. These seniors who had appeared larger than life now became human. They reminisced about how they had gone through a similar ordeal just three short years ago and encouraged each of us to persist until the end. I could somehow sense a feeling of sadness behind their stories, knowing their time at Texas A&M was nearing an end.

Celebrating throughout the afternoon, we returned to the dorm somehow feeling a little taller than we had been a few hours ago. As we entered the dorm with our new senior friends, the sophomores and juniors wasted no time in letting us know we still were subordinate to them. They immediately informed us that we had yet to drop handles with their classes, and continued to hammer us about our freshman responsibilities.

We walked a thin line for several days, knowing the end was near, but wanting to remain unified as a class and avoid any unnecessary conflict. The more we appeared unified as a team, the quicker the rest of the upperclassmen would drop handles with us.

Within two weeks we received word of the junior drop handle crap out. This time we were only given a couple of hours advance notice. The word quickly spread to the rest of the fish. Having made it through the senior crap out, our confidence level remained high.

Nothing could break our spirits as we again scrambled out into the hallway for the crap out with the junior class, this time wearing sweat suits and combat boots. It started with the usual class set of push ups and was followed by some tag team races up and down the hall.

We were then told to "bust butt" outside for a little outfit jog. The juniors had apparently decided to run us to death and, after what seemed like about ten miles, eventually lead us to a secluded park where we dropped handles with each of them, similar to that of the seniors. We again celebrated our achievement and received some much needed advice from the junior class. We were informed that the sophomores were upset that we were no longer taking them seriously. They were going to make life miserable for us until we showed them the respect they expected.

"Until you guys straighten up," Mr. London said, "they're going to continue to treat you guys like dirt."

We were tested to no end the following week. The pissheads looked for any opportunity to make us push. They tried every trick in the book to cause disharmony between us.

"Are you sure you want to be a sophomore?" Mr. Brown asked me one morning prior to chow.

Knowing he was trying to trick me, I quickly responded with "Mr. Brown, sir, fish Quinn requests permission to make a statement, sir."

"Go ahead," he said.

"A fish is not allowed to want, sir."

"You've come a long way, fish Quinn," he said.

It was then that I made my last fatal mistake as a fish. I said "Thank you, sir."

A fish is never allowed to tell a sophomore "thank you" because of an incident that had taken place several years earlier during the building of the Aggie bonfire. As a group of cadets were loading a huge log onto a flatbed truck, the log broke loose and rolled back toward the cadets. A sophomore pushed a freshman out of the path of the falling log; and the sophomore was killed in the process. Because the freshman never had the opportunity to thank him, we were still never to say the words "thank you" to them.

"Did you hear that?" Mr. Brown hollered to the other sophomores in disbelief. "Fish Quinn said, thank you! Why did you go and do a stupid thing like that, fish Quinn?"

"No excuse, sir!" I responded, knowing full well I had screwed up, yet was amused that he had put me on the defensive.

"Everybody drop!" Mr. Brown yelled. "Push until I get tired!"

As we pushed, I could here chuckles from the sophomores standing overhead. This was what they were looking for, a final opportunity to display their vanishing authority, knowing it would soon be over. Actually, I felt no real remorse. I had indeed come a long way in a short period of time. Just a few months earlier, I was simply a freshman at a major university. Now I was about to become a sophomore in the Corps of Cadets at Texas A&M and guide-on bearer of Squadron Two. What more could a fish want?

As we continued to push, I began to question my preparedness. Could I really lead others? Were we prepared as a class? Were we really ready to teach and train others? Would I ever wear a pair of senior boots?

So many questions yet to be answered ran through my mind. I was certain about one thing: this is where I wanted to be. I knew that when I graduated from Texas A&M, my education would consist of much more than mere text book learning. It would be a combination of experience in discipline, team work, unity, leadership and accountability. The Corps was teaching me how to overcome obstacles. It was teaching me about commitment. I felt like a sponge, absorbing it all. I was becoming engulfed in the Corps and what it represented. It consumed my every thought. I had gradually become a part of something larger than myself. Something that no one could ever take away from me, and it felt great!

CHAPTER 10

THE LAST CRAP OUT

Our relationship with the sophomores grew uncomfortably tense as final exams approached. It was difficult for us to remain obedient to them while on a first name basis with the junior and senior classes. The pissheads continued to increase the pressure as a constant reminder that we had yet to drop handles with them.

During this period of time, I gained a special respect for those freshmen who had persisted since the first semester. I had missed a lot of what they had been through and admired their perseverance. Because of the pressure of the Corps, several of our classmates would not be returning the following semester. I realized that it took a special kind of person to voluntarily subject themselves to this kind of ordeal for nine months while carrying a full class load. It took someone with an extreme amount of foresight and, perhaps, a bit of senility.

Simply making it through the Corps was a tough enough road, but we were also expected to make decent grades. After all, that was the main reason for attending Texas A&M.

Jumper and I would often discuss how we envied our friends outside the Corps who enjoyed a nice apartment with no additional responsibilities. We didn't really understand why we were putting up with this rigid lifestyle, but something inside kept telling us to hold on. A common spirit within, a small glimmer of hope somehow kept us hanging on.

The big day finally came. I was in Probst and Roosma's hole discussing the upcoming year when the door flew open without warning. There stood Mr. Reed, a six foot, six inch sophomore who weighed more than 200 pounds.

"You three have five minutes to be out in the hall in fatigues, combat boots, outfit shirt and hat," he said in a commanding voice. "Every second you're late will mean another class set of push ups for your fish buds. Any questions?"

"No, sir!" we replied.

I scrambled back to my hole where Smiley was already changing. We joked as we prepared, knowing full well the next couple of hours would be pure hell, but we were ready; as a matter of fact, we actually looked forward to it. After this crap out we would no longer be fish.

"What can they do to us that the juniors and seniors haven't done?" I asked as we raced to get our boots tied.

"Don't underestimate the pissheads," Smiley responded. "They're bound to have something up their sleeves."

Fish Probst and fish Roosma were running behind as usual when we filed out into the hall to join the rest of the freshmen.

"Go get your fish buds, Quinn," Mr. Dugat yelled.

I ran down to Probst and Roosma's hole and found them frantically searching for something.

"Hurry up, you guys," I said. "The pissheads are really getting hot!"

"We can't find Probst's belt buckle," Roosma said.

"Quinn," Probst wailed, "if you have anything to do with this, so help me, you're dead."

"All right," I confessed, knowing time was critical. "Look in the left pocket of your rain coat. Now hurry up and get out here!"

"You're dead, Quinn!" Probst threatened.

"In your dreams," I snickered as I returned to join the rest of freshmen in the hall.

"Stop where you are and push until your buddies get out here, fish Quinn!" Mr. Cain yelled as I stepped back into the hall. I did so, dropping in front of Probst's door.

"Look who's dreaming," Probst whispered as he and Roosma stepped over me.

"Everybody drop and give us a class set!" Mr. Tevis commanded. We began, but were continuously stopped and told to start over for not counting together as a class. After several attempts, we were finally allowed to complete the class set. After a lengthy lecture on class unity, they allowed us to get up, then ushered us outside and told us to form up for a little "joy run." We began by running across campus, jodying along the way.

"Probst," Mr. Goff hollered, "it's your turn to jody!"

"Oh, no," I thought to myself. "Probst likes to make up his own jodies as we go. I hope he doesn't get us into more trouble." Suddenly the inevitable rang out.

"Tacos and razor blades!" Probst began.

"Knock it off, Probst!" Mr. Ingram yelled. "That ain't funny! We'll run all day if you guys don't straighten up."

We were directed off campus and were told to drop for another class set. Once completed, we were teamed up with our old ladies for wheelbarrow races. With Smiley holding me up by my legs, I lunged forward, attempting to run on my hands. We traded places at the finish line. I grabbed Smiley's legs, and he began the return trip on his hands. I apparently pushed too hard, forcing Smiley head first into the dirt. I landed on top of him to the amusement of the sophomores.

"Get up!" Mr. Reese commanded. "Let's go!"

We formed up and began to run again. After about a mile, we approached what looked like a small pond.

"You fish run through the water," Mr. Day ordered as the sophomores veered to the side. Smiley and I concluded the water looked pretty good and decided to dive head first into it to cool off. Together, we hit the water and disappeared beneath the surface. We came up gasping for air.

"You guys stink," Mr. Black laughed.

What had looked like water was, in actuality, some sort of sewage pond. We rose from the muck, amidst the laughter, and attempted to wipe the gunk from our faces. The rest of the outfit avoided Smiley and me during the remainder of the run due to the smell emanating from our clothes.

After several more miles, we finally reached a secluded area with a small lake. Here we finally dropped handles with the pissheads. It was sheer ecstasy. I'm sure it was just as much a relief to the sophomores as it was to us; they were ready to become surgebutts and were tired of trying to keep us in line.

One by one we were introduced to each of them, by first name, then thrown into the lake. For Smiley and me, it was a welcomed exchange and gave us an opportunity to rid ourselves of the awful odor we had acquired earlier.

We celebrated the remainder of the day and enjoyed the opportunity to joke with them, but took care not to take it too far. They were still upperclassmen, but for at least a short moment, we felt like their equals. We eventually returned to the dorm where the entire outfit was now on a first name basis and were given steam shower privileges by the juniors. We took it as an opportunity to bask in our success.

"Man," I told Smiley as we entered our "room," I never thought I would see this day.

"Me neither," he said as we headed toward the shower. "It don't get any better than this."

That night we all met at Sparkey's to celebrate our success and survival of our fish year in the Corps. We freely spoke of the trials we had endured throughout the year, along with many of the memorable moments. One of the most memorable events was our march to the Brazos with the rest of the Corps. We did this as a fundraiser for the March of Dimes campaign. We had marched seven miles to the Brazos River to take part in various competitive events with other outfits like tug of war, stretcher races, and potato bag races. Each event was refereed by actual members of the Dallas Cowboy Cheerleaders.

After the events, the juniors and seniors were allowed to return by car, while the sophomores led us on the return seven mile trek by foot. This is where Probst had gained the reputation for making up the worst jodies in the history of the Corps of Cadets. We also laughed about the time a junior from another outfit had made a critical remark about our outfit. His comment, commonly known as a "fart off," eventually caused him grief. We were ordered by one of our juniors to "take him to the quad." Taking someone to the quad was a common form of retaliation from one junior or senior to another. Our fish class followed orders and headed over to the other junior's dorm. Wearing only our shorts, we surrounded his room and waited. After finally realizing there was no escape, he reluctantly surrendered.

We escorted the junior cadet back to our dorm where several buckets of water awaited him from two stories up. We laid him down on the cement steps outside of our dorm door, then held his legs open and poured several 55 gallon trash cans of water on him from the second floor. Quadding has a way of teaching a cadet not to criticize another outfit.

The Fish Drill Team often took individuals to the quad, but dropped the water from four stories up instead of only two. Needless to say, rarely did anyone "fart off" the Fish Drill Team.

We also laughed that night about how we probably looked like idiots during cush races. After each evening chow, we were given a specific type of cush, or dessert. When cream pie was served, it was tradition to see which fish could finish his piece first. During cush races, we were not allowed to use our hands. Each freshman would first identify which piece belonged to him by sticking his finger into it. The pieces would then be distributed as we waited with our hands behind our backs. Once the signal was given, we would attempt to eat the pie without hands. The first to finish would place his plate, upside down, on his head. The winner would normally receive some kind of special privilege, which often made the race tempting to win.

"How are we going to tell our future wives about all of this?" fish Jumper asked as we laughed until it hurt.

"I'm not sure I'll want her to know," Garrett said. We all eventually decided it really didn't matter because no one would believe it anyway.

We returned to the dorm that night, anxious for Final Review which was now only days away. In a blink of an eye we would change from fish to pissheads. I was nervous because, as the new guide-on bearer, I was required to create and perform an original series of special moves with the guide-on during the second review. I had practiced hours upon end, trying to create interesting maneuvers.

The world around us had changed dramatically during the last few weeks. We had actually made it. All that remained now, assuming we all passed our final exams, was Final Review. After that, we would be pissheads and all we lacked was a new freshman class to whip into shape!

C H A P T E R 1 1

FINAL REVIEW

The quad was buzzing with excitement as family and friends gathered on the quad prior to Final Review. Many parents had themselves taken part in the same tradition years before, and it was obvious they were excited for the opportunity to witness a son or daughter do the same. The Corps dorms were opened to visitors and the normally stringent rules were relaxed for the weekend.

Smiley and I arose and put on our fish uniform for the last time. We would march with our outfit once as freshmen, then return to the dorm to don our sophomore uniforms, never again to be addressed as "fish." The sophomores would in turn change into their new junior uniforms, white belts and all. The juniors would slide on their newly polished senior riding boots, signifying the ultimate cadet accomplishment.

As we initially formed on the drill field, the seniors began shaking hands with each member of our squadron. Appreciation was expressed by all classes for the leadership we had received from this class of seniors. We knew their influence would continue to be felt for years to come.

"Bingo Baby!" Dale Lane shouted as we were brought to attention by the Corps Staff. This was our commanding officer's official trademark which we all recognized.

Suddenly, the Aggie Band pierced the silence with the *Aggie War Hymn*. Chills ran up and down my spine as I felt the spirit, pride, and the sense of accomplishment swell within me. Only now did it really begin to set in. I had made it. One time around the drill field and I would be a pisshead, something only a fish could appreciate.

"Forward, march!" Dale commanded as we stepped from our formation for our final review.

There's something about the sound of the Aggie Band that makes a fish walk a little bit taller. It somehow makes all of the sweat and struggle worth the effort. There are never any words that can describe the feeling, and it's often difficult to explain to those that have never been through the experience of being a fish in the Aggie Corps.

We had just rounded the first corner when Mr. Tullos yelled, "Let 'em know who we are, Gators!" We instinctively tightened our formation and prepared for our final review before the military officers.

"Squadron, eyes right!" Mr. Lane commanded for the last time. It felt for a moment as if the world stood still just for us. We were each somehow saying, "Look at us, we made it!" Each cadet had overcome several personal obstacles in order to get to this point. Each had made numerous sacrifices along the way. For our fish class, it was only the beginning. When our hands dropped, we would be pissheads.

"Squadron," Mr. Lane began. "Ready, front!"

We snapped our heads back to the forward position and dropped our salutes in unison. It was over almost as quickly as it had begun. We were pissheads!

The seniors immediately wrapped their arms around each other on the front row. From where I marched, I could see heads drop and I knew tears were falling.

I began to wonder how I would react when my turn came, if I ever made it that far. My grades had slipped after I had joined the Corps, and I knew I had my work cut out for me.

"Surely I won't cry," I thought to myself. "It can't mean that much."

We marched from the drill field and extended our thanks amidst hugs from the seniors, then turned to leave. I felt a strange sense of sorrow for the seniors as we headed back to the dorm. My emotions were short lived, however, as I became excited about the thought of what was about to happen. We would return to the dorm and change into our new sophomore uniforms for the second review.

The seniors waited behind for the new Corps to appear without them. They would now stand on the side lines cheering on the new leaders that they had developed during the last three years.

We returned to the quad and into the dorm to change. Fish Neese raised his fist high into the air and yelled, "Pissheads, yea!" The rest of us joined in with a "whoop!" Though it was actually only a junior's or senior's privilege to "whoop," no one said a thing to us. Everyone seemed to be lost in the excitement of their own world. Once in our "room," which we were now permitted to call it, Smiley and I changed, then looked over the other's uniform. We were slightly unsure of ourselves, for we had never actually worn a sophomore uniform before. This would be the first time we would not be inspected prior to a formation.

"Don't forget the guide-on," Smiley reminded me as we started to leave.

"Thanks," I said. "We'd look pretty stupid without the guide-on, especially today."

I unlocked the chains that held it to a water pipe in our room. We kept it locked, keeping it safe from the upperclassmen who often tried to steal it from us.

I reviewed the various guide-on maneuvers over and over in my mind as we marched back to the drill field for the second review. It seemed strange to be marching out in front of the outfit with Steve London, our new commanding officer. His pride was evident by the shine emanating from his senior boots worn publicly for the first time today. I knew it had taken months of work to prepare the shine and, again, wondered if I would ever get a chance to wear a similar pair. Jumper also led the outfit carrying our newly awarded athletic flag.

Our outfit was smaller in number, now that we had no fish. It would be the only time during the year that the entire Corps would march without a freshman class, since everyone had been promoted.

After several pictures from relatives, we formed up. I felt the familiar chill run up my spine as the band struck up the *Aggie War Hymn* for the second time that day.

We stepped off, full of excitement, and rounded the drill field behind Squadron One. We made our final turn toward the reviewing stand.

"Are you ready, Dan?" Steve asked as we neared the officers on the stand.

"I guess so," I responded, slightly unsure of myself. "I just hope I don't hit you."

We had practiced the guide-on maneuvers together to the point that we knew it took exactly 22 steps to accomplish. "Squadron!" he hollered, giving me the signal to begin the maneuvers.

I stepped to the left, and twisted the blue and gold outfit flag over my head in a counter clockwise position. I then pulled it behind my back and up the left side of my body. I could hear Steve quietly counting as we approached the reviewing stand. From a distance I heard our old seniors cheering us on from the side of the drill field. I twisted the guide-on over my right wrist as Steve reached the count of eighteen.

"Eyes, right!" he shouted.

I snapped the guide-on to its final position in front of the reviewing stand. The military officers returned our salutes as we passed before them. I couldn't believe it had actually worked! As we passed the reviewing stand, I held the guide-on, relieved that it was finally over.

"Looking good, Gators!" someone shouted from next to the stand. "Squadron, ready, front!" Steve commanded as the squadron dropped their salutes, and I returned the guide-on to its upright position. The seniors followed from the side lines and met us at the end of the drill field as we completed the march. I was amazed at how excited they were for us. I could see the pride beaming from their faces.

"You guys will always be my fish!" Mr. Lane shouted as we marched past him on the way back to the quad, "and don't you ever forget it!"

It was over. We were finally full-fledged pissheads! What a relief. I wondered what the coming years would bring as we marched across campus back to the quad.

"What would our new freshmen be like?" I silently pondered. "How would we as a class function now that we had earned a little bit of freedom? Would we remain unified? Would we be able to gain the respect of the new fish class?" Suddenly my thoughts were interrupted.

"How does it feel to be a pisshead, Dan?" Mr. Ingram asked. I almost responded with the instinctive fish answer of "Sir, it's not a fish privilege to feel." Realizing it was now my privilege, I simply said, "I'll let you know next year, Bob, when I catch me some fish."

CHAPTER 12

PISSHEADS!

I loaded my belongings on the Greyhound bus in College Station and headed north to Arkansas for the summer. My high school friends back in Arkansas found it difficult to understand my experiences during the previous five months as I told them story after story about life in the Corps of Cadets at Texas A&M. They were shocked to see my hair so short, remembering how I had worn it fairly long during high school.

Summer break back home was a nice change of pace after the hectic semester. I worked as a stock boy at a local Wal-Mart throughout the summer to earn extra money for the upcoming year. By the end of August I was rather anxious to return to A&M. I had made several wonderful friends, in and out of the Corps, and was looking forward to seeing them again. Before I knew it, I was saying good-bye to my parents again. And, thanks to Dad, I acquired an old Chevy Malibu to take back to school.

I headed south for another one of many long, 12-hour drives to A&M. I had been selected as a Fish Camp counselor prior to the summer and left a week early in order to spend a few days at camp with a new class of freshmen. I rolled into College Station on a warm, breezy Sunday evening, feeling excited about the upcoming year. The contrast between being a freshman and a sophomore seemed to make all the difference in the world.

I parked near our new dorm and began to haul my belongings into my room. Mike Probst and I had decided to room together this year, and he, too, had been selected as a Fish Camp counselor.

"Howdy, fish Quinn," he said with a big grin as I entered the room with a hand full of clothes.

"Howdy, Mr. Probst, sir!" I responded in jest as I slammed my body up against the wall. We shook hands and chatted about the summer break, then began organizing our room.

"Seen the new fish yet?" he asked.

"No, have you?" I answered.

"Yea."

"How many are there?"

"Twenty."

"That's a pretty good group," I said. "Think we can whip 'em into shape?"

"No problem," he answered with a grin. "I've already met a few of them. Andy wants us to stay away from them for a while, until he gets them used to the Corps."

We tried to avoid the new fish as much as possible that night. They were still going through "F.O.W," or Fish Orientation Week, which was designed to get them accustomed to the numerous rules of the Corps. They were being taught by Andy Reese, one of our juniors, who had volunteered for the task. It was best to keep them away from all upper-classmen until they had learned how to formally "whip out."

The next morning, Probst and I gathered with the other fish coun-selors at the MSC to prepare for Fish Camp. We met our freshmen, who consisted of both men and women who would attend Texas A&M the coming semester. Most of these freshmen were not affiliated with the Corps of Cadets.

Fish Camp was, again, a great experience, and it allowed me the opportunity to become good friends with a lot of students I would have never met otherwise. It was my chance to give back a little of what had been given to me the previous year. This time, it was I who explained the traditions at A&M during the bus ride. I could see the look of con-fusion in the expressions I received from several of the new students as we traveled. I knew they didn't understand what I was trying to tell them, and I remembered my initial impression of the traditions at Texas A&M. I did my best to explain what it would mean when they finally found out what being an Aggie was really all about.

Three days later, we returned to the campus, all somehow a little bit better. Probst and I said good-bye to our new friends and walked together to the quad where we would be known by 20 new fish as "Mr. Quinn" and "Mr. Probst." I had made up my mind to do whatever was required, in order to become a senior in the Corps and to experience Final Review as a zip. I still couldn't really fathom the opportunity. It remained a dream that loomed somewhere off in the distant future. My immediate task lie a few hundred feet away from us in the form of a bunch of freshmen who had just left a life of leisure. They were all probably wondering, about now, why in the world they had joined the Corps.

As Probst and I entered the dorm, we were greeted by several of our former "fish buddies" who were visiting with each other in the hall.

"Howdy, pissheads!" Ogdee said.

"We've been waiting for you guys to get here so we can go get some pizza." Roosma added.

"Hey, we don't even have to get permission!" I said with a smile.

After greeting each of our classmates, we headed off to discuss the upcoming year.

"Have you seen the fish yet?" McAnally asked. "They're scared senseless. Andy's told them we're all a bunch of animals."

"Does it look like we have a pretty decent athletic class?" I asked.

"Yea. They should have a good chance of holding on to the freshman sports flag we won last year," Jumper responded.

After pizza, we headed for the Dixie Chicken. This was the classic Texas Honkey Tonk, complete with swinging doors, ceiling fans and antique artifacts which covered the walls. It even held a built-in snake pit, complete with live rattle snakes. It was a favorite gathering place for students looking for a place to relax and socialize.

We renewed acquaintances and discussed what we, as sophomores, expected of ourselves and from the new fish. We established goals and decided to go easy on the fish until they had been given adequate time to become accustomed to the many rules and regulations. We were not allowed to get too friendly with them, as we were expected to be leaders. It was now our job to teach them discipline and teamwork.

We would also be expected to remain unified as a sophomore class. If the freshmen were to detect conflicts within our own ranks, they would surely take advantage of it. We had been warned by the new junior class that we were still not above being crapped out if they deemed it necessary.

I relished the first semester of my sophomore year in the Corps. It gave me the opportunity to experience several events I had missed during the first semester of my freshman year. Time seemed to fly by as I became acquainted with our fish class, one by one. They worked hard at learning the ropes and soon learned that teamwork took priority over individualism.

We enjoyed our new found freedom as pissheads, though the juniors tried to continually tighten the reins. We were continually reminded of the fact that we were actually only glorified fish and would have no real freedom until we became "white belts," which signified advancement to the junior rank.

The job of a pisshead is never an easy one. We were often caught in the middle and pressured from both sides. The juniors were constantly on us to increase pressure on the freshmen class and took every opportunity to expose their every flaw to us. The fish, on the other hand, didn't care for us a great deal either, as we were constantly on their backs trying to get them to work together as a team. We soon found out that we were definitely not the most popular cadet class in the Corps, but did our best to keep everyone satisfied.

Since I had missed the first semester of my fish year within the Corps the previous year, I was expected to catch up on several "character building" experiences. One was the making and wearing of fish spurs. During the week prior to the annual football game between the Aggies and the SMU Mustangs, all fish are expected to make spurs out of coat hangers and bottle caps. Since I had missed the experience, I, too, had to make and wear spurs. I fitted the make-shift spurs with 81 bottle caps. Bottle Cap Alley was the ideal location to acquire the needed number. This is where thousands of bottle caps cover the ground in an alley next to the Dixie Chicken.

For an entire week prior to the SMU game, I was required to wear the spurs everywhere I went, including class. I received numerous stares from the regular students as I walked across campus making a clanking sound with each step.

Football season brought with it the annual Aggie bonfire prior to the game between the Aggies and the Longhorns. Several Saturday mornings we rose at day-break, loaded the freshmen on flat bed trucks, and headed out to a thick patch of woods. There we would cut down trees to be burned in the bonfire. Each outfit staked out a plot of land from which they would cut and haul several huge tree trunks back to the flat bed trucks for the return trip to campus. Log after log was carried carefully from the cutting sight by each outfit. The loading process was done with extreme caution; one false move could be fatal, as had occurred in the past.

The building of the bonfire seemed to become the catalyst for the unification of our new fish class. The teaching of teamwork was intensified during this period of time, as each relied upon the other for its accomplishment. Bonfire became for us a symbol of commitment and achievement. The pride and gratification felt at its igniting is only understood by one who has sweated and sacrificed, alongside others, day after day, night after night. "Red Pots" directed each phase of construction. This awesome responsibility rested with these elite cadets who practically lived at the construction site on campus. As a matter of fact, they built a log cabin on the sight, which gave them a place to eat and rest during the building. They devoted hour upon hour to insure each log was placed and wired correctly. The bonfire was constructed and wired together in a tier shaped fashion, resulting in a safe and adhesive fall, once ignited.

I watched with a renewed sense of appreciation the night the bonfire was lit. The yell leaders, red pots and Aggie Band circled the huge stack of timber several times, holding their torches high above their heads. Finally, each threw his torches onto the structure as we watched in amazement. As the fire rapidly grew, the Aggie Band began to play. The crowd let out a loud "whoop" as the *Aggie War Hymn* started.

The experience became larger than life when Jumper turned to me and said, "This is what it's all about, Quinn. Feels good, doesn't it?"

"I've never felt anything like it before!" I hollered above the sound of the band.

To me, the flames represented achievement. Achievement by a group of strangers who had been brought together by chance, but had become friends by choice. I knew the lesson of commitment learned here would be a foundation we would all draw upon for the rest of our lives. Bonfire also meant the end of the mental war that our freshmen had waged with our commanding officer, Steve London.

Eighty-two days prior to the lighting of bonfire, our fish had stolen all of Steve's belongings, including his clothes. They removed everything from his room, even his senior boots. He returned from class one day to find his room void of all possessions. There was no bed, no desk, no books, no phone ... nothing! It quickly became a contest of will to see who would give in first. The fish wanted to keep his belongings hidden until the night of bonfire. This would show the ultimate achievement in class unity.

Steve made life miserable for the fish by requiring them to memorize every upperclassmen's home town and major field of study at A&M. They were also forced to sleep in their rain gear each evening and to "duck walk," or walk while squatting, whenever they were in the dorm. There were many other little "inconveniences" designed to make the fish class surrender and return Steve's belongings to him prior to bonfire.

It was tradition for all other upperclassmen to stay out of the struggle; it was strictly a battle between the fish and the Commanding Officer. This little war made things easier for us in a way, as we were not forced to continually discipline the freshman during this period of time.

Eventually, the pressure became so great that the fish began to bargain for removal of certain restrictions. They were allowed to sleep without rain gear for the return of Steve's senior boots and the books he needed for class.

It is the ultimate test of endurance for either party to maintain decent grades while withstanding the adverse pressure from the ordeal. The freshmen could be seen studying in unusual places all over campus, in an attempt to avoid having to return to the dorm to face Steve. Eventually, the fish class gave way to the pressure, and returned the remainder of Steve's belongings to him just prior to bonfire.

It took no time at all for things to return to normal, and we were soon back to being the bad guys again. When discipline was needed, we tried to keep the crap outs to one hour or less. We were never allowed to touch a freshman, which helped everyone maintain control of their emotions. We could scream our heads off if we chose to, but were we to touch even one fish, we would have gone too far and the repercussions would have been serious.

The most important aspect of any crap out is knowing why it is being done. Usually, it was brought about by one or two fish pulling out privileges they had not yet received. Though I understood their perspective, I was now on the other side of the fence. It was my job to catch them. When we did catch them, we would often request that the guilty individual watch as the rest of the class did push ups for him. It didn't take very long for the peer pressure to persuade everyone, even the most stubborn cadet, to follow the rules.

The juniors and seniors were somewhat removed from the discipline

process and acted as mediators, insuring the freshmen understood what
was going on. These freshmen would spend the next three years with us
and, one day, would replace us. We wanted to make sure they understood the meaning behind the discipline process. Without discipline, the
Corps would have been chaotic.

It's a difficult task as a pisshead, to balance the new-found freedom
acquired, with the responsibility we had over the freshmen. As other
interests entered each of our lives, it became increasingly difficult to concentrate on our Corps responsibilities. It was during these times that the
juniors reminded us that we could still be crapped out if they felt we
were neglecting our duties. As a matter of fact, they did crap us out once
during our sophomore year. The fish were restricted to their holes and
were not able to witness the event. After the crap out we improved our
focus on the task at hand, realizing we would have two more years in
which to devote time to other activities, like girls.

As the year neared its end, it now became my duty to select the next
guide-on bearer. I selected fish Gardner, a small, but dedicated, fish
who had always seemed to get the job done when the chips were down.
He had a great desire to carry the guide-on and, as we ran our initiation
run around the golf course, we stopped at each corner for a class set of
push ups as I had done a year earlier. As his arms shook from fatigue, I
encouraged him to give it all he had. I reminded him of his duty to
carry the guide-on before the outfit during march-ins and outfit runs.

We finally returned to the quad for our victory lap. This time my feelings were not of pride in myself, but in fish Gardner. This time, it was
my fish who had made it. I somehow sensed what he was feeling. I
knew he was a different person now. I knew it and he knew it. He was
ready and he deserved to carry the guide-on for Squadron Two. We
stopped in front of the dorm and I handed him his guide-on.

"Congratulations, fish Gardner," I said. "It's all yours now."

"I'll guard it with my life, sir," he answered.

"You better, because I know some pissheads who want it, too."

"Mr. Quinn, sir," he began before I even completed the sentence.

"Rest!" I said. "I know deep down you know what a pisshead is.
Now get in the dorm and shower. You smell like sweat."

"Yes, sir," he said with a smile.

CHAPTER 13

SURGEBUTTS!

As had happened with us only a year earlier, the opportunity to drop handles with our fish had arrived. We felt a sense of accomplishment to see them finally unify as a team. They had finally learned to depend on each other. Final Review was fast approaching, and I could sense their excitement and anticipation of becoming pissheads. We, on the other hand, had only one thing on our minds ... becoming surgebutts! I had been told, as a fish, that the Corps would take on an entirely different meaning once I had the opportunity to wear a white belt, signifying the upperclassmen from underclassmen. I don't recall who had said it, but he was right.

As we marched for the second time during Final Review, it seemed like an entirely different Corps of Cadets. The first two years had come and gone as if it had all happened only yesterday. Suddenly, we were one step behind the seniors, in white belts and all. We were now responsible for providing the majority of leadership to the outfit. It didn't seem possible, but we had somehow made it. We said good-bye to another senior class and made a commitment to work closely with the new seniors. They wanted to enjoy the next year with us and needed our help in making Gator Two the best outfit possible.

I had only recently decided to accept a commission as an officer in the Air Force after graduation and was assigned to attend Officer Training Camp, a mandatory four-week training period, at Lackland Air Force Base in San Antonio that summer. Both Roosma and Probst were assigned to attend the same camp in August, meaning we would all be in San Antonio at the same time. How this occurred, I hadn't the slightest idea, but I did have a feeling we were in for a memorable summer camp.

I drove from Arkansas to Memphis, Tennessee, then flew to San Antonio in the middle of August for camp. The heat and humidity hit me like a warm, damp towel as I stepped from the airplane. From the airport, I took a bus to Lackland Air Force Base and was escorted to the barracks where my assigned flight was located. I quickly became acquainted with several of the other members of "India Flight" and shared backgrounds with each of the other officer candidates. Our barracks appeared to be of World War II vintage. Without air conditioning, I knew even the evenings would be hot and uncomfortable.

I quickly made my bed (military style) and assisted several others who had never seen it done before. Most of the cadets were attending a university or college where ROTC was simply a way to get into the Air Force. To most of these cadets, their military curriculum meant one ROTC class per week and an occasional drill. The vast majority of these cadets had never been required to polish shoes or even to learn how to march. The Air Force officers in charge somehow had been informed in advance that Aggies liked to sleep on form fitted sheets, to avoid having to remake their bed each morning, so they required us to sleep under the sheets. We were actually inspected several times late at night as we slept to ensure we were not sleeping on top of the covers.

Each morning, we were awakened at 5:30 for our daily mile and a half run, after which we would shower and prepare for morning chow. Because of the humidity, the perspiration would begin during the morning run and normally continue throughout the remainder of the day. We drenched uniform after uniform as we marched in the hot, humid, 110 degree South Texas weather. At times, it became so hot that a red flag would be raised in several locations on the base, signifying the heat had reached the danger point. During these times we were to remain indoors. Several cadets were from the northern part of the United States and were not accustomed to this sort of heat and humidity. Because of this, there was always the danger of heat exhaustion and dehydration.

My most memorable moment of summer camp occurred at approximately 10,000 feet above the ground while pulling five G's. We were each given a back seat ride in a T-38 training jet as part of the Air Force four-week orientation. While accomplishing a loop, the G pressure (gravity pressure) became so great that I "grayed out." As we performed the maneuver, the pressure from the maneuver had forced the blood from my head causing me to lose my vision for approximately 20 seconds. My peripheral vision eventually returned when the pilot finally leveled the jet.

"How do you feel?" the pilot asked over the intercom.

"Great," I responded. "Can I try that?"

"Well," he said. "We're getting kind of low on fuel. We'd better get back to the base."

Upon landing, I thanked the pilot and returned to the training area. Though I had no desire to become a pilot, I figured if I could swing a few rides like that one every now and then, it would indeed be worth it for me to accept a commission after graduation and enter the Air Force.

I managed to successfully complete the Air Force training and was even allowed to lead the flight through a "fancy" drill competition during the final week of camp.

After graduation from summer camp, I returned to Arkansas for the remainder of the summer, spending most of my time again at the local Wal-Mart stocking shelves and chasing shoplifters.

My 12-hour drive between Arkansas and Texas A&M was now becoming routine. I figured I would make the trip at least 18 times prior to graduation. This year my return trip was different. I looked forward to finally becoming an upperclassmen and receiving $100 per month as part of my Air Force ROTC incentive for joining the Air Force upon graduation.

"I'm going to be rich!" I told my parents as I loaded up my car and prepared to head south. "How am I going to spend a hundred dollars a month?"

"Ever thought about saving some of it?" my dad asked as I pulled out of the driveway.

"Nope!" I responded as I drove away. "See 'ya at Christmas!"

College Station was a again a welcomed sight after the long, hot drive. The huge campus had become a familiar place and felt more like home with each passing year. Everything in the Corps became a joy. Knowing we now wore white belts relieved us of the day-to-day pressures we had experienced previously as freshmen and sophomores.

We were now expected to be the mediators of the outfit. It was our job to make sure the sophomores whipped the fish into shape. On the other hand, we were also to give the freshmen encouragement when they felt like throwing in the towel. We were also expected to solve the majority of problems in the outfit, allowing the seniors the opportunity to have as much free time as possible.

One of our most cherished of all junior privileges was the steam showers. Each evening, several members of our class would congregate in the large shower and run the water up to a scolding hot temperature, causing the steam to build into a thick fog. Amidst the hot water and steam, we would discuss the day's events, good and bad. Many important decisions were made while relaxing in the steam shower each evening. The temperature would eventually become so hot, we would have to open the window to catch a breath of cool air.

Smiley had become the first sergeant of the outfit, which meant he would most likely become our Commanding Officer the following year. He took his position seriously and, at times, struggled to keep the rest of us from becoming too apathetic about our obligations within the Corps. It was tempting to forget our responsibilities, now that we had so much freedom. We could come and go as we pleased and were pretty much allowed to do whatever we wanted, as long as we took care of our specific outfit duties. Though we were not exempt from room inspection, we were given the opportunity to alter the appearance of our rooms. Many added a split level effect and lush carpets, giving the small rooms the appearance of some elaborate penthouse suite. I suppose, to some extent, this helped remove the memories of our barren fish holes we had been forced to keep spotless only two years earlier.

I became the "A" flight officer with Ogdee as the "B" flight officer. Our primary responsibility was to teach the freshmen how to march. We were also to insure the outfit marched effectively as a team in preparation for the various march-ins and competitions that we would participate in. We also conducted the freshman and sophomore marching competitions between the cadets in our outfit. Day after day, we worked at teaching the freshmen the expected drill maneuvers they would need to know in order to compete. They eventually became fairly proficient and did well in the competitions.

I enjoyed the Corps more and more as time progressed and the numerous associations made only enhanced my satisfaction at my decision to have joined. Brian Yates, another junior, had recently transferred to our outfit from another squadron and became a valuable asset to our unit. We were again in pursuit of the Corps Sports Flag as an outfit, and he added to our athletic endeavors.

Probst and I were again roommates and had made a joint decision to become waiters at Duncan Dining Hall for some additional spending money. We rose each morning, earlier than normal, donned our white waiter jackets and headed to the chow hall for table preparation. Probst had developed a bad habit of sleeping through his alarm, so he had fastened two separate clocks to his bed with boot straps. The first clock was designed to arouse him from his deep sleep, then several minutes later the second one would ring and, supposedly, wake him completely. I would often rise at the first alarm, silently dress and sneak out without waking him. He would usually oversleep, then scramble to the chow hall just in time to assist.

"Why didn't you wake me up, Quinn?" he would always ask as he stumbled into the dining hall, still trying to get his waiter jacket on.

"Gosh, I tried," I would normally respond, "but the bag monster must have gotten you again."

The "bag monster" was a fictitious creature in the Corps that mysteriously forced cadets to oversleep.

Probst and I continued our pranks on each other. One evening, while studying, I told him I had seen a UFO land somewhere in the middle of campus.

"You're lying," he said, as I hung out of our fourth story window pretending to determine the exact location of the landing.

"No, really," I said. "I saw bright lights swirling around in the sky, and it landed over behind Rudder Tower! I've read about some recent sighting in the area. I'm going to go get a closer look!"

"I'm not buying it, Quinn. It's another one of your stupid jokes," he said with disgust, as I quickly put on my shoes and ran from the room.

I darted down the hall and ducked into Roosma and Ogdee's room and hid in their closet, hoping he would think I had left the dorm. I then heard Probst scrambling to get his shoes on. Suddenly, he ran down the hall, past the door, and scurried down the stairs and out of the dorm. Roosma, Ogdee and I ran to the window in time to see him running across the quad toward the middle of campus.

Barely able to contain my laughter, I finally hollered, "Hey, Probst! Where are you going?" Instantly realizing what had actually occurred, he ducked behind a bush to hide. Hearing our laughter from the window, he attempted to return to the dorm undetected, darting from bush to bush hoping no one would see him. By now, several other cadets had heard what had happened and were watching from their windows. We chuckled as he tried to make his way inconspicuously back to the dorm.

Everyone applauded as he finally entered the room.

"Quinn," he said. "I'll get you back if it's the last thing I do."

"I hope I'm around to see it," Neese said as he left to return to his room. "That should be good."

It wasn't long before Probst did get his revenge. At about three a.m. on a cold February morning, I was rudely awakened by our entire fish class and carried from my bed to the showers where a stream of cold water awaited me. I was held down while a thin stream of cold water pelted me between the legs.

"Happy birthday, old lady," Probst said as he watched from the door in amusement, knowing I was helpless.

"Happy Birthday, Mr. Quinn, sir!" the fish said in unison as they finally let me rise to my feet.

"I guess this means we're even," I said to Probst as I stooped over in pain.

"Only if you're lucky," he chuckled with a sinister expression as he handed me a dry towel.

Our escapades never really interfered with our deep- rooted friend-ship. Our late night discussions of school, the Corps and, of course, the hottest male topic on any college campus, girls, often lasted well into the night as we shined our senior boots in preparation for the following year. The dream of one day becoming seniors drew nearer and nearer as the year went on. We were eventually given permission to wear one senior boot in the hall each evening between 9 and 10 p.m. This privi-lege had a dual purpose. The first was to allow us the opportunity to break in the tough leather and adjust our feet to the fit of the boots. This would help us avoid blisters the following year. The other reason, and most significant, was to give each of us a taste of what lie ahead for us. The seniors knew we would work harder for them if we actually got a small taste of becoming a zip.

During the fall of my junior year the urge to compete in elections for one of the three senior yell leader positions began to consume my every thought. Ever since I had met the head yell leader my freshman year, I had dreamed of one day leading the band into Kyle Field, with torch held high, for midnight yell practice. There were five yell leader posi-tions in all, two junior slots and three senior positions. Two of the three senior positions available were usually filled by the two incumbent junior yell leaders who would run for re-election. This meant that there was, in reality, only one senior position that would probably be filled.

Each yell leader position, along with all other student body positions, would be voted upon by the student body after a designated two-week campaign. The senior yell leader positions were open to all students who had obtained enough credits to be classified by the university as seniors the following year, both male and female, in and out of the Corps. Being a member of the Corps had both its advantages and disadvantages. The advantage being that every cadet was strongly encouraged to vote, and each cadet would probably vote for a Corps candidate. The disadvantage was that all potential Corps candidates were to meet and choose among themselves, only two new seniors receiving official Corps sponsorship in the elections. This was done to give all cadets a choice without dispersing the cadet votes over a wide range of Corps candidates.

There were approximately twenty juniors within the Corps interested in the senior yell leader position, and we met several times socially to become acquainted with one another. Mark Outlaw and Ed Franza, the two incumbent junior yell leaders, attended these gatherings also. They were almost assured of re-election and answered our many questions about the requirements of the position. They informed us that, because of the visibility, we would be ambassadors for Texas A&M wherever we went. Our conduct would have to be respectable at all times, as we would be watched continuously, not only by the students, but by former students, faculty and university administrators. Should our conduct become unbecoming, we would be reprimanded and could possibly loose the position.

After several meetings, we were each asked to cast a secret ballot containing our top two choices for official Corps sponsorship. It was mutually agreed upon that only the two chosen from the group would run against all other university candidates, including Outlaw and Franza. My heart pounded the evening the final vote was turned in. I watched intensely while Outlaw and Franza counted the secret ballots that had been passed to the front of the room.

"Looks like we've got our two candidates," Outlaw finally said.

"As your name is called, we'd like for you to come forward," Franza added in his low, rough voice.

"Rick Fairchild," Outlaw announced.

A tall, stout cadet walked to the front of the room amidst claps and cheers from the other candidates.

"Well," I thought to myself, "that probably does it for me." I had just about given up all hope when Franza called out the second name. Before I knew it, people were congratulating me on being the second selection. He had called my name! As I walked to the front of the room, my mind instantly began to reel with ideas on my campaign.

"Could I possibly win?" I wondered. "How could I get people to vote for me? I don't even know the moves to the yells. How was I going to learn the moves to each yell in time to campaign?" My thoughts were abruptly interrupted as Outlaw and Franza shook my hand.

"Congratulations," Outlaw said. "Get your campaign ready, and we'll see you two after spring break," Franza added. "And good luck to you both."

I returned to the dorm wondering how all of this had happened. Would I really lead the Aggie Band into Kyle field for midnight yell practice? Would I stand at mid- field with the football team prior to the first home game next year against Penn State? Surely not," I convinced myself. "But maybe, just maybe ..."

CHAPTER 14

FROM FROG
TO ZIP

I prepared for the yell leader campaign first by recruiting Probst as my campaign manager. We spent our spring break at his home in Baytown, painting campaign signs on his driveway. A week later we returned to A&M and, much to my amazement, the designated areas were already filled with numerous campaign signs from various other candidates. Several individuals from outside of the Corps had also decided to run for senior yell leader.

I soon learned that, outside the Corps, the majority of voters would come from the coeds on campus. I decided to target the Corps and coed voters first, then, if time permitted, solicit the remainder of the dorms on campus.

The two weeks of campaigning consisted of speaking engagements, interviews and door-to-door solicitations. Day after day, I went from one dorm or meeting to another, introducing myself and asking for votes. Throughout the campaign I was invited into rooms and offered the opportunity to display my proficiency as a potential yell leader and asked to perform specific yells. I was a bit hesitant at first, but realized that some embarrassment was part of the calling. I found it easier to do if I could persuade those in attendance to perform the yell with me. They were usually willing to do so and often called friends from other rooms to join in the fun. The rooms would soon fill, as others came to see what all of the commotion was about. Eventually, I overcame my embarrassment and became fairly proficient at the movements to each yell.

The two weeks of campaigning seemed like two months. I was relieved when election day finally arrived. As I walked with my outfit to the voting booth, the outfit joked about how no one was going to vote for me.

"It'll sure look funny if everyone else gets thousands of votes and Quinn gets one," Probst chided as we walked.

"And the one will be his own!" Roosma added as the outfit began to laugh. "Listen up, fish. No one is allowed to vote for Quinn. Got that?"

"Yes, sir!" the fish class responded in unison.

"Cute, Roosma." I said, trying to hide my nervousness.

After voting, we were informed that the election results would be posted later that evening on the doors of the Memorial Student Center. I found it impossible to concentrate on my studies that afternoon, knowing the results would soon be posted. As I reviewed my text that evening for an upcoming quiz, my thoughts drifted back to the day I had been dropped off at A&M for Fish Camp. The fear and insecurity I had felt as a freshman had gradually been transformed into a confidence I may never have achieved without the discipline provided by the Corps of Cadets. I wondered what the last three years would have been like, had I not joined the Corps. Time slipped by as I tried to imagine what lay ahead.

Suddenly, my solitude was shattered when the door flew open and Jumper yelled, "Someone said the results have been posted! Let's go!"

I leaped from my desk and together we darted down the hall and out the door. We ran across the campus towards the MSC with nervous anticipation. We arrived and scurried up the stairs to the doors where the results were posted. Quickly, we began skimming the numerous pages, searching for the yell leader results. I found the page and noticed that Mark Outlaw had accumulated the most votes. I then saw the name of Ed Franza listed next. My heart skipped a beat as I continued down the list comparing votes.

"You did it, Quinn!" Jumper hollered as he glanced over my shoulder.

"Are you sure?" I asked as we re-examined the figures.

"Yep!" he replied as he held one hand high.

"Congratulations!" he said as our hands met with a loud clap. "You're a senior yell leader!"

"Holy smokes!" I clamored. "What do I do now?"

"Celebrate!" Jumper exclaimed. "What else?"

He treated me to pizza that evening as we celebrated and talked about the upcoming semester. He had become a member of the Ross

Volunteers that year and, while stuffing our faces with pizza, we laughed about the times when, as fish, we would imitate their unique march in the halls. We had both accomplished goals we had set as freshmen and now looked forward to our senior year with great anticipation.

The following evening, the newly elected yell leaders met with the out-going senior yell leaders at Sparkey's to formally exchange positions. After some much needed advice, we were then given the formal initiation. Needless to say, my derriere was extremely tender for the next couple of weeks.

The eventual approach of Elephant Walk gave us, as a junior class, the opportunity to let the seniors know we were finally ready to take charge of the outfit, whether they liked it or not. We referred to ourselves as "zips" throughout the preceding week, refusing to yield to their warnings of punishment. Initially, they shuddered at the fact that we were uttering the most sacred of all unspeakable words prior to officially obtaining the rank of senior. We knew it was too late for them to do anything about it, though we were careful not to rib them excessively in front of the underclassmen.

Elephant Walk finally arrived, and a massive line of seniors gathered at the flagpole on military walk to begin their final stroll around Aggieland. As in years past, male and female seniors participated from both in and out of the Corps. As juniors, we simulated their massacre while the several hundred students walked the campus. We dressed in an array of battle attire and hid like snipers in the trees as they approached the quad. When our class of seniors passed beneath, we jumped from the trees and covered them with a net. An old fashioned brawl immediately erupted and the long awaited wrestling match began. For approximately thirty minutes we rolled through the dirt, mud and grass with each class trying to overcome the other. After a vigorous match, they finally surrendered and agreed to meet us later to celebrate the informal exchange of power.

Later that afternoon, we celebrated our three years together. We laughed now about events that were deadly serious a few years ago, like during crap outs when Mr. Hale used to make us catch those #!*#!* butterflies in the steam showers.

For our seniors, the end was near. Final Review now loomed on the horizon as their final hurrah prior to graduation. For us, it represented the beginning of everything we had worked to achieve over the last three, long years. We would finally have the authority to come and go as we pleased. We could say what we wanted, sleep in late, "drop handles" with the food and, the ultimate of all senior privileges, walk on the grass in our senior boots. These privileges would not be treasured by any other college senior but, for us, it was like returning to heaven. It represented our arrival and, for me, the completion of a long and, at times, difficult journey through the ranks of the Aggie Corps, from frog to zip.

Final Review my junior year was a dream come true. As we marched around the drill field for the second pass in our freshly shined senior boots, the pride beaming from the front row of new zips was eminent. The outfit was finally ours now. We had truly arrived.

"Who would have ever believed it?" McAnally asked, as we completed our pass and marched off the field. "After this, what's left?"

"Elephant Bowl," I replied.

I spent the following summer at Texas A&M attending summer school by day and working at the Dixie Chicken bussing tables at night. I also had the opportunity to participate in freshman orientation programs throughout the summer. These orientations gave incoming freshmen and their parents a better understanding of Texas A&M and its traditions. There were usually between two hundred and three hundred students and parents in attendance each evening in the Rudder Tower auditorium. My part of the program was to explain the origin of yell leaders and to actually demonstrate several yells.

Each evening, I would ask the entire audience to stand and participate, even requiring the parents and grandparents to wildcat after each yell. A good time was had by all and it gave me additional time to overcome my nervousness about the new position. While I was assisting with the orientations, Outlaw was busy practicing with the A&M football team. After a series of interviews he had been selected as the head yell leader which placed him formally in charge. Tradition has it that the head yell leader attend pre-season practices with the Aggie football team throughout the summer, up until the inter-squad scrimmage which takes place just prior to the start of school. Outlaw was often asked to hold the blocking dummies while the running backs attempted to flatten him, and often did.

I envied Outlaw for the opportunity he had to associate with the team on this level, yet pitied him at the same time as the heat, humidity, and torridness of the hot Texas summer was almost unbearable. Rain was badly needed and the heat exceeded 100 degrees almost daily during the summer months.

I roomed on campus with Jumper through summer school, and we often returned from class and crawled out our window onto a hot, rock-tarred roof to tan. We had created a fictitious beach complete with lawn chairs, towels, and music. Each afternoon we basked in the sun discussing the upcoming year completely unaware of the heat blisters slowly forming on our bodies.

We often played our guitars and sang Beach Boys tunes, amusing those who passed by. I'm sure many thought we were a bit senile, but we were oblivious to it all. We were officially zips and the world was ours. We felt victorious and consumed the very essence of the moment.

Time stood still for us that summer as we absorbed not only the sun, but the feeling of accomplishment. We were enjoying the downhill slide of a long and grueling climb to the top of the Corps, one that had taken us from strangers, simply struggling for survival, to the best of friends rejoicing in the realization of what three years ago was simply a fantasy.

We also became avid supporters of three friends who had decided to ride their 10-speed bikes from San Antonio to Canada that summer. Bobby Jenkins, David Hime and Matt Burns had decided to attempt the feat, calling us periodically throughout their northern trek. The final victory call eventually came one evening at approximately 2 a.m. from the Canadian Mounties, informing us they had indeed reached Canada. I told them it had only been six weeks since their departure and would only believe it when I saw the pictures.

As all good things do, the summer came to a conclusion. By now, we were anxious to don the senior cadet uniform and to assume our new responsibilities within the Corps. Jumper had recently earned a position on Corps Staff, a select group of seniors chosen to lead the Corps each year. I was proud of him, as he was of me. We both took our positions seriously and committed to giving it every thing we had.

My senior year finally became real the night we surprised the new Corps fish class with a secretly pre-planned midnight yell practice. I, along with the other yell leaders and members of the Aggie Band, waited at the South end of the quad at midnight and laughed as the new class of fish were suddenly aroused from their sleep and hustled out of the dorms. They were then directed toward our location and appeared from the darkness like bats exiting caves in the black of night. Within seconds we were surrounded by several hundred screaming cadets. Still only half awake, they continued to wildcat and awaited further instructions.

"Hump it, Army!" Outlaw finally hollered as we held the gig'em sign high above our heads. Still confused and disoriented, they bent over. As we performed the movements to the yell, their voices thundered across campus in unison with the beat pounded out on a bass drum from the Aggie Band. The pulsing voices pierced the silent night and shook the very ground where we stood.

We took opportunities between yells to tell jokes and attempt to motivate these new cadets about the journey they had recently decided to embark upon. I knew what they were thinking and could feel their apprehension, but knew it would all disappear after the next song.

I felt that familiar tingle as we stood erect and began to sing *The Spirit of Aggieland*. We led the hymn before hundreds of wide eyed fish, now beginning to beam with excitement and pride. I'm sure they didn't fully understand what was happening, but I was certain they would never forget it. I stared intently into the eyes of the fish as we began to sing:

Some may boast of prowess bold,
of the school they think so grand.
But, there's a spirit that ne'er be told,
It's the spirit of Aggieland.
We are the Aggies, the Aggies are we.
True to each other as Aggies can be.
We've got to fight boys, we've got to fight.
We've got to fight for maroon and white.
After they've boosted all the rest,
Then they will come and join the best.
For we are the Aggies, the Aggies are we.
We're from Texas A.M.C.

As we continued, I witnessed the entire cluster of cadets mysteriously change during the course of one song from a group of strangers, recently thrown together during fish orientation week, to the Aggie class of nineteen hundred and eighty-four. They were now a part of a new team, one that would rely on each individual to pull his or her own weight. Their high school accomplishments meant nothing any more. Each would be expected to prove himself again within the Corps just as every cadet over the last hundred years had done.

We disbanded after the song and each outfit returned to their separate dorm. We assembled our new Gator fish in the hallway and each senior took the opportunity to express his feelings about Texas A&M and the Corps of Cadets. We told them it was going to be hard. We tried to prepare them for the tough days, the days they would feel like quitting. We did all we could to encourage each cadet to stick it out, to see their decision through to the end, for one day they would also wear the senior boots and have the opportunity to return the favor to a future class of freshmen. We promised them, though they could not see it at the time, that it would all be worth it one day. For now, they would just have to believe us and survive each day, one at a time.

As full-fledged zips, we finally had the opportunity to sleep in during morning formations, since only a single senior was required at morning formation. It was pure heaven to roll over each morning while the whistle blew for morning chow. For three long years I had waited for this opportunity and, finally, it was here. No mandatory early morning uniform inspections, no daily room inspections, no wildcatting ... it was wonderful.

During meals we could now sit where we wanted, eat as much as we could hold, and address the food by its proper name.

"What more could a person ask for?" I thought to myself as I sat to eat for the first time as a zip.

It felt strange to sit in the same seats the last three classes of seniors had occupied. It didn't seem possible. They had somehow seemed larger than life and, now, here we were — a bunch of nobodies acting like we knew what in the heck we were doing.

It seemed like only yesterday that Mr. Day was chewing me out for not taking those stupid fish bites.

The first stroll in my senior boots felt peculiar as I walked to class for the first time my senior year. Several months of polishing had gone into their shine. They fit securely over my riding pants, rising to a point just below my knees. We wore symbolic spurs which caused a slight clinking sound as we walked. We had learned to recognize this sound as freshmen, warning us of approaching seniors and the potential for another whip out.

The first yell practice of the year had been planned for Monday evening in G. Rollie White Coliseum. The entire football team, along with the coaching staff, would be in attendance. As we entered, I could see the entire arena was filled to capacity. It was an exciting moment, as I had never been in front of a crowd this size before. I was nervous and worried that I would forget what I was doing and that someone in the crowd would notice my mistakes. I could see it now. The campus newspaper tomorrow would read, "Senior yell leader screws up during first yell before thousands!"

Actually, it turned out to be a blast. I felt a strange sense of power as the entire coliseum shouted in unison to each of our movements. Even the football team and coaching staff accompanied each yell.

"What would it feel like out on Kyle Field?" I thought to myself as I gazed out at the crowd as they yelled. I wondered how loud it would be when the Aggies made their first appearance into the newly remodeled football stadium. A third deck had recently been completed. I had experienced several occasions over the past three years when the games were delayed because of the noise level the crowd created. I could hardly wait!

Our first football game was scheduled to be played in Mississippi against the Rebels of Ol' Miss. Because of mechanical problems, our plane was delayed from the Dallas/Fort Worth Airport, and we were not able to reach the game until late into the second quarter. My family had driven from Arkansas to attend the game and were in attendance when we finally arrived.

I had watched several major collegiate football games from the stands, but had never been able to watch one for any length of time from the side line. The excitement and electricity that occurs on the field is, at times, indescribable. I had never fully realized the intensity at which major collegiate teams played. This was serious stuff. I saw several news reporters caught in the line of fire and smashed, as huge, barbaric linebackers drove their targets out of bounds into the turf, fully intent upon leaving them there.

The Aggies were victorious that evening and returned to College Station the following day. Upon return, we gave our white uniforms to Mike Thatcher, one of the two junior yell leaders. It was his responsibility to make sure our uniforms were cleaned and pressed prior to each game. Chris Walker, the other junior, was responsible for our finances. He was to ensure we had our tickets, transportation and spending money taken care of prior to each away game.

At Texas A&M, rank hath its privileges, and since our two junior yell leaders were part of the class of 1982, they were also required to carry 82 cents worth of change with them at all times. This requirement was conjured up in case a senior yell leader wanted something during a game. The change was taped to the inside cover of a small book containing Aggie traditions and was to be carried with them at all times. If the money was spent, it would have to be replaced prior to the next game. Our pangs of hunger occurred at the strangest times, requiring the juniors to quickly return with food and drink.

We chartered a small plane to Atlanta for the next football game against the Georgia Bulldogs. Unbeknownst to us, Georgia had recently acquired an unknown freshman running back by the name of Hershel Walker. I can remember early in the game seeing this freshman break through the line for a 76-yard touchdown run.

We were out-scored 42 to three that day. Georgia went undefeated and eventually won the national championship that year. The Aggies returned to College Station a bit humbled, but had no time to dwell on the past. They had only one week to prepare for the first home game against Joe Paterno and his Nittany Lions. Football at Aggieland ... I could hardly wait!

CHAPTER 15

MIDNIGHT YELL PRACTICE

My older brother, Bill, and a friend of his named Larry, had driven all night from Jonesboro, Arkansas, where they were attending Arkansas State University to witness a midnight yell practice and to attend our first home football game against Penn State. I had attempted to describe the activities at Aggieland several times during my trips home, and he had decided to find out if it was everything I had described.

They arrived early on a Friday morning and were directed to my dorm just prior to morning chow. One of our fish escorted them to my room where Probst and I were preparing for morning inspection. Bill was a little perplexed at the way the freshmen carefully kept their right shoulder up against the wall as they walked in the hallway.

"You make these guys call you Mr. Quinn?" he asked, as they entered the room.

"We had to do it when we were freshmen," I responded as we shook hands. "It builds character."

He chuckled, then introduced me to his friend, Larry, and said, "There's a guy out there with his back up against the wall. Does he have a bad back or something?"

"No," I laughed. "He's just at attention. He's announcing the menu for morning chow."

"Why are they walking with their shoulder up against the wall?" Larry questioned.

"They're fish," I said. "We can keep track of them better that way. They're just following the rules."

They watched intensely as the fish were inspected by the sophomores prior to morning formation.

"You had to go through all of this?" Bill asked as several freshmen began to do push-ups.

"Yea. It's not so bad once you get used to it. It really keeps you on your toes."

"Looks like you make these guys spend a lot of time on their hands," he responded with a look of amusement as we left the dorm for morning formation.

We marched to chow while Bill and Larry followed from behind. They were a little apprehensive about eating with us after watching the pre-meal festivities in the hall. They looked at each other in disbelief as our table was quickly prepared and the freshmen asked for permission to be seated.

"What kind of drugs do you have these guys on?" Bill asked as the freshmen began asking for food.

"Just a little dose of pride," I responded with a smile.

"What makes you guys want to go through all of this?" he asked.

"You'll probably get your answer tonight around midnight," I said, referring to midnight yell practice. "We should get a pretty good turn out. We're hoping for around 30,000 people."

Bill turned and looked at Larry with an expression of doubt. At approximately 11:30 that evening we met behind the Corps dorms with the Aggie Band, along with several hundred students, to light our torches in preparation for our first midnight yell practice of the year. We huddled together for a short prayer, then lit the torches. Arm in arm, the students assembled behind the Aggie Band as our torches went up in flames. A loud "whoop" followed as the band pierced the night with the first few notes of the *Aggie War Hymn*.

Hundreds of sophomores lined up around us and the band, linking arms, preventing anyone from breaking rank. We stepped forward with our torches held high overhead and began our stroll to Kyle field. We waived to Dr. Koldus, Director of Student Services, as we passed his house on campus. He stood on his front porch with his wife as we passed, offering a smile and a wave. Bill and Larry followed from the side, staying within eyesight of us. I wanted them to experience yell practice from down on the field and knew if I lost sight of them I might lose them in the crowd.

As we approached the stadium, I could see the stands overflowing with people. I motioned for Bill and Larry to join us as we entered the dark concrete tunnel leading to the football field. The noise level in the stadium increased as it echoed through the tunnel toward us. We entered the stadium with our torches held high as the crowd clapped in unison to the beat of the Aggie Band. We doused our torches in a huge bucket of water to the right of the tunnel and turned to face the crowd, signaling for them to increase the noise level. The energy within the stadium was incredible.

The band, along with their dates, remained in formation and marched the length of the field. As they returned to the north end zone, I, along with the other four yell leaders, made a mad dash around them to the 50-yard line. During this run to the middle of the field, Outlaw, Franza, and I attempted to tackle the junior yell leaders. Having them outnumbered was a definite advantage, but they managed to get in several good licks of their own. We targeted Thatcher and, in a matter of seconds, had him on his back. Once at mid-field, we made the juniors do push ups while the Aggie Band continued to play.

At the conclusion of the band's first number, we knelt and huddled together, forming a tight circle in the middle of the field. After discussing what only yell leaders know is discussed, the juniors again performed additional push ups in sync with the beat of the Aggie Band.

From the middle of the field, I could see the lower deck almost entirely filled with people. Several hundred others were watching from the second deck. I couldn't believe that this many people had shown up.

We waited for the music to stop, knowing that when it did, the juniors would make a mad dash for the side lines, trying to avoid us. This time, our primary target was Walker. As the music ended, Walker tried to use Thatcher as a screen, attempting to run around us. Franza eventually caught him by his overalls, and they both tumbled to the artificial turf. This was all in good fun, and they knew that they would probably get their turn next year when they became senior yell leaders.

We each took our assigned spot on the track that surrounded the football field as Outlaw gave the signal for the first yell. Thousands of hands mirrored the signal in the stands, ensuring all in attendance knew which yell to perform. Each person in the stadium leaned forward into the "hump it" position as we counted to three. In unison, the student body shouted the words that correlated with each of our moves.

Up until tonight, I had only heard the yells from within the stands as part of the crowd in Kyle Field. I hadn't realized it would be so loud from out in front. I now understood why opposing teams had been known to practice during the week with Aggie yells blasting from loud speakers in preparation for their games at Aggieland.

Aggies have been known to use this unique form of crowd control to their advantage as often as possible, at times making it very difficult for opposing team members to hear plays or signals being called by the quarterback. I have also seen the noise take its toll on opposing coaches, often causing confusion on the visiting side lines.

After a couple of yells, we sang the *Aggie War Hymn*. Outlaw then told an amusing story over the loud speakers. These "groad stories," as they are called, are another unique tradition at A&M. During the early days of the school, the yell leaders told stories to the rest of the cadets while on the steps of the YMCA building located on campus. We carried on the tradition in the stadium by acting as if we were walking up steps and rolling up our sleeves while telling these stories.

Following Outlaw's story, Thatcher received his opportunity. He concluded his story by saying "Beat the class of 82 hell out of Penn State!" This type of remark was only reserved for seniors. By saying it at yell practice, all juniors in attendance were required to drop for a class set of push ups. We counted as Walker and Thatcher pushed along with the thousands of other juniors in the stadium. After completing the push ups, the stadium lights were turned out, allowing all in attendance to kiss their dates ... if they had one. Those without dates lit matches or lighters and held them high above their heads signifying their loneliness.

The *Spirit of Aggieland* was the final song played. It seemed to put the final touches on the first yell practice. Bill and Larry stood there in awe as the student body shouted each word of the yell portion of the hymn.

"Man, you guys don't fool around, do you?" he said as the yell practice concluded. "I've never seen anything like this before."

I thought about his comments as we left the stadium and wondered just how this whole thing had become such a huge tradition. It was hard to believe that a hundred years ago, the late night activities of a few cadets in the middle of a deserted Central Texas prairie would eventually culminate in the largest on-going university assembly in the world. This, along with all of the other traditions at Texas A&M, is what made it unique.

I saw students, parents and grandparents walking together from the stadium, three family generations brought together at midnight by something grand. Something called the "Aggie Spirit."

"This is crazy," Larry said as we walked back to the quad. "If the yell practices are like this, what are the games like?" he asked.

"Just wait," I said. "You ain't seen nothing yet."

C H A P T E R   1 6

MARCH IN!

Iwas awakened by the sound of feet stumbling down the stairs. I rolled over and reached for my alarm clock in the darkness. It was only 5:30 a.m. Then I remembered it was game day at Texas A&M, and our squadron had been assigned to post several flags around the campus prior to sunrise. Football at Texas A&M is more than just a sporting event; it's a passion. At Aggieland, football is a sport in which everyone participates, not just the athletes on the field. For us, it meant an early morning run followed by formation and our first march-in of the year. It would be our first opportunity as a zip class to wear our senior boots on the front row in Kyle Field.

The excitement I felt as we prepared for the game and march-in was almost beyond control. Because of my nervousness, I had slept little the previous night. This would be the first football game to be played in the expanded stadium, now holding more than 70,000 spectators.

After the morning run, we showered and prepared for formation. Parents and relatives were milling around the quad early to meet with sons and daughters who would participate in the pre-game activities.

We assembled on the quad with the rest of the Corps and greeted old classmates and friends who had returned to the campus for the game. It was not uncommon to find several former Corps members on the quad at any given moment in time, reminiscing about their collegiate days at Texas A&M. You could easily spot them with their wives and children, pointing, trying to describe what was happening during each phase of the festivities.

Our sophomores immediately began inspecting the fish as we fell out for formation, looking for anything that might resemble a "pull out." On this occasion, the freshmen had tried to hide pieces of sophomore insignia by pinning it to the inside of their biders. This, of course, was definitely against the rules. They were soon caught by the sophomores and told they would pay for it the following week. The excitement was evident on several pisshead faces, knowing they now had their first legitimate reason for a good, old fashioned crap out.

Smiley brought the outfit to attention, ending the commotion. He reminded us that we would be judged and scored by the active duty officers, or "bulls" as we called them, from the moment we stepped from the quad until we had passed the reviewing stand inside the stadium. He glanced over the outfit one last time for anything amiss, then turned to report. After each outfit had reported, we were given the signal to "hump it."

The Corps has a unique way of expressing its pride, it's called, "Corps, hump it." After each cadet was in a crouched position, the count of three was given. At the count of three, several thousand cadets shouted in unison, "The fighting Texas Aggie Cadet Corps! The Twelfth Man! The spirit of Aggieland! The best damn outfit anywhere!" This of course, was followed by each class wildcatting in their own peculiar way.

Suddenly, a loud explosion pierced the air. A nearby cannon had been fired by the Parsons Mounted Cavalry, surprising the several hundred spectators on the quad. The band played the *Aggie War Hymn* as we began our unified march to Kyle Field. As we took our first steps, the juniors and seniors let out a loud "whoop!"

My brother looked at me with one of those "you've got to be kidding" looks again. I could see the eyes of the freshmen light up as they caught a glimpse of why they were here. I knew that after this day they would be much better prepared to carry on, regardless of the obstacles ahead. I sensed this event would somehow help solidify our unit. We marched down the street, passing hundreds of onlookers that filled the sidewalks to the stadium. Several juniors jodied as we marched, while the sophomores kept an eye out for any fish that might be out of step with the rest of the outfit.

It felt a bit unusual to finally march with the other seniors on the front row. I never actually believed this day would arrive. Time had gone by so quickly.

We finally stopped outside of the north entrance to Kyle Field and separated into two lines on each side of the road. As the Aggie football team and coaching staff entered the stadium between us, we held a mini yell practice for them. Several freshmen from each outfit were chosen to lead the Corps in these yells. I chuckled as they attempted to keep their balance while performing the maneuvers.

Once the team had entered, we marched to the corner of the stadium in preparation for the review. The Aggie Band led the way as each outfit waited their turn in nervous anticipation. Finally, our turn came. Once on the soft track, it was difficult to keep everyone in step. The rubber surface suppressed the sounds of our heels, so we were all dependent on the beat of the band for our cadence. As we approached the reviewing stand, someone yelled out, "Bingo, baby!" Only those of us on the front row knew who it was — Dale Lane, our C.O. during our fish year, was in the stands cheering us on.

We saluted the military staff as we passed the reviewing stand, our cadence in sync with the beat of the band. After a return salute, we continued our march to the end of the stadium. Once off the track, I separated from the outfit and headed toward the locker room to change into the traditional white yell leader uniform. As I entered the locker room, I could tell the suits had been recently cleaned and pressed, thanks to Thatcher.

"You do good work, Thatch," Franza joked as we began to change. "Can you have all of my other uniforms pressed like this?"

"Yea, if you pay me enough," Thatcher said in jest.

My heart began to pound as we exited the locker room and walked down the narrow passageway toward the opening of the stadium. The sound of the crowd intensified as the echoes danced down the tunnel toward us. The feeling was everything I had dreamed it would be, and more.

As we reached the entrance I said a silent prayer, "Lord, thanks for this day and, please, don't let me screw up in front of all of these people!"

Kyle Field looked larger than I had ever remembered, as we stepped out onto the track. My eyes slowly adjusted to the bright afternoon light. It was perfect football weather — warm with a slight breeze from the south. I glanced back to look at the crowd and was amazed to see the stadium at near capacity. As I stared at the colorful mass of humanity, I could barely see the faces of those on the third deck. We had nick named it the "nose bleed" section because of the altitude.

My life suddenly flashed before my eyes as I was almost trampled.

Joe Paterno and his Nittany Lions entered the stadium fully intent upon running me over. I felt like a midget in a land of giants as they passed. They were apparently out for revenge, for we had upset them at Penn State just two years earlier when they were nationally ranked and heavily favored.

We took Reveille and joined the Aggie football team at mid-field for the coin toss. Reveille, our university mascot, was a female collie and the highest ranking cadet on campus.

"Call it in the air!" the head referee hollered above the noise, tossing the half dollar up.

"Heads," the Aggie team captain yelled with confidence as the coin twisted in the air, seemingly in slow motion.

We watched intently with the captains of Penn State as the coin returned to earth, finally settling on the turf. "Heads, it is!" the referee shouted. "Do you want to kick or receive?" he asked the Aggie captain.

"We'll receive," the player said, signaling back to the Aggie bench.

As the referee announced the results of the coin toss, the entire Aggie team came onto the field in preparation to sing *The Spirit of Aggieland*. Thatcher and Walker ran to the sideline while Outlaw, Franza, and I remained at mid field with Reveille and the Aggie football team. Photographers surrounded us, snapping pictures of Reveille as she barked to the beat of the Aggie Band. Once the song started, something engulfed me. My attention turned inward. It seemed as though I had suddenly entered an illusion. Never in my wildest dreams did I ever think I would be standing in the middle of Kyle Field with the entire football team helping kick off an opening game like this. I didn't want the song to end. My adrenaline increased and my heart pounded as the football players joined in with the student body to sing and yell. The noise level was incredible. The Penn State players turned to look at the crowd as if to say, "What have we gotten ourselves into?"

At the conclusion of the song, the blast of a cannon sounded, bringing me back to reality. We led Reveille off the field and headed to our assigned locations on the side lines.

It was a memorable game and, though we were out-scored (Aggies never really lose), I shall never forget it. Along with the student body, we remained after the game for an additional yell practice. We felt partially responsible when the Aggies were not victorious and felt it was everyone's duty to practice the yells again before leaving the stadium in order to improve prior to the next game.

Our first home victory found us soaking wet in the Fish Pond afterwards. With approximately three minutes left in the game the Corps fish began to file out of the stands like hungry buzzards. Eyeing their prey, they surrounded the field in anticipation of the final cannon blast that would signify the end of the game. I knew this meant being chased, tackled and carried across campus to the Fish Pond where I, along with the other yell leaders, would be thrown in. I handed my valuables, including my wallet and shoes, to Pam, my date, for safe keeping.

As the cannon sounded, I made a mad dash for the center of the field. I wasn't really sure which way to run and figured I could decide once I got there. Halfway across the field, I was blind-sided by a rather large cadet and suddenly found myself tumbling across the turf. The next thing I knew, I was on the bottom of a pile of fish, hardly able to breath. I was eventually lifted high above their shoulders and carried out of the stadium.

"Hey, no pinching!" I ordered as they carried me out of the stadium.

"Yes, sir!" they laughed, continuing anyway.

Once at the Fish Pond, I was lifted high into the air and tossed into the water. I can remember thinking the water looked deeper than it actually was and felt a jolt of pain as my rear end hit the cement below the surface. I was sore, but I couldn't let the fish see me in pain. So, I arose out of the water with a huge artificial smile on my face, cursing them all silently beneath my breath.

I was soon joined by the rest of the yell leaders as they were thrown in one by one. We led the fish in a few yells while still in the Fish Pond. When the band arrived, we climbed out of the water and moved over to the steps of the YMCA building where the midnight yell practices had taken place so many years ago. There we held another short yell practice and took turns telling groad stories.

We traded places with the drum majors and led the Aggie Band in a hymn as they took turns leading yells. After a joyful time, we returned to the quad to dry.

As the year progressed, I became more familiar with the duties and obligations of a senior yell leader. One of the most honored duties was the lighting of the annual Aggie Bonfire. The student body, under the

direction of the Red Pots, had put in several months of preparation leading up to the event. As with the previous years, the task was monumen-
tal and involved several tons of timber.

On one particular gloomy, stormy Sunday afternoon, Roosma and I
found ourselves the sole workers on the huge structure. We carried one
log after another to the theme song from the movie "Patton" blasting
from the outdoor speakers. We were cold, wet and tired, but enjoyed
every second of it.

We chatted about what bonfire represented. There were some who
felt it was simply a waste of time and resources, but we disagreed. There
are some things in which only those who participate can fully understand. We knew without a shadow of a doubt that bonfire was an integral part of the development process that brought us together as a team
and would be remembered long after the ashes were gone. To us, bonfire meant unity, responsibility, teamwork, accomplishment and pride.
Other charity work should be, and is, performed by the Corps and the
rest of the student body, but bonfire should never be eliminated.
Without it, Texas A&M moves one step closer to becoming just like
every other University, void of its tradition and uniqueness.

The night finally came to ignite the mass of timber and wire that had
been carefully constructed. The outhouse, which represents t.u., had
been placed earlier that day high upon the top. Amidst the cold rain
which had begun, we lit our torches with the Red Pots and leaders of
the Aggie Band. We circled the bonfire twice as the Aggie Band played,
holding our torches high. We waded through the cold mud, as it had
rained earlier that day and the temperature had dropped to almost freez-
ing. We then tossed our torches onto the huge structure and watched in
amazement as it quickly lit up the dark night.

What had taken months to build was now ablaze and would fall within minutes. We stood in awe of the huge blaze and all that it represented to us as Aggies. I watched as the structure began to groan, twisting
under the intense heat and pressure. The logs had been carefully wired
together, causing the stack of timber to fall within a predetermined
radius. Snow began to fall as the bonfire collapsed, crashing to the
ground.

The Red Pots stood arm in arm as they watched. For these men, the
massive blaze represented more than just fire. It stood for commitment.

Commitment to something they would always remember. They had devoted several months to its construction and had accomplished an enormous task, one that few would willingly accept while carrying a full class load.

As I turned to head back to the dorm, a faint melody pierced the Texas night. I turned, and from the vicinity of the bonfire, could scarcely make out a group of Red Pots, still arm in arm, humming *The Spirit of Aggieland*.

I somehow sensed what they were feeling, for we had all felt something similar at one time or another while at Texas A&M. It was something impossible to explain, yet as tangible as the ground I stood on. It was what made A&M unique. To me it was an inner spirit, one that seemed to echo the voices of the countless Aggies that had given their lives for their country in defense of freedom. Because of their numerous sacrifices, I was being given this opportunity. I was not only appreciative, I was proud — proud to be an American and honored to be an Aggie.

CHAPTER 17

AUSTIN, HERE WE COME!

O nce every other year the Corps of Cadets invades the capital city of Texas. Not literally, of course, for we love our capital as much as any other Texan. We simply march down the city streets of Austin on game day, usually ending with a short yell practice on the steps of the capitol building. Parson's Mounted Cavalry, the cadets on horseback, followed the rest of the Corps during these march-ins, for obvious clean-up reasons.

These excursions are called Corps trips. Each class of cadets within each outfit normally spends the previous night at a classmate's home in the area. These trips sometimes turn into late night parties, making it difficult to rise and prepare for the march-in the following morning. Inevitably, someone forgets a portion of his uniform, causing fear of embarrassment within the entire class. This paranoia is magnified within the freshman class, knowing the entire class would suffer should some-one forget anything.

The Corps trip to Austin my senior year was sweet indeed. We defeated the Longhorns in Memorial Stadium, surprising most in atten-dance. One particularly humorous event occurred during the second half of the game. It seems t.u. selects an elite group of men each year who are responsible for a huge cannon used during the game to signify each Longhorn score. These individuals are normally dressed to the hilt in cowboy attire, chaps and all. Apparently, part of their responsibility is to protect the cannon at all times, knowing Aggie cadets will try any-thing once.

During a particular lull in the game, we were all startled with the sound of a huge explosion. I turned to see what had happened and observed a cloud of white smoke rising from the cannon. Three fresh-men cadets were running out of the stadium with several high stepping cowboys close behind in hot pursuit. Other cadets then began to jump from the stands in support of their fish buds.

I surmised that several of the cowboys had walked to the front of the cannon in order to obtain a better view of the game. Three Aggie fish, recognizing the opportunity, had run past and fired the cannon. I'm sure the cowboy's ears were ringing, not to mention what may have occurred in their pants, as they frantically chased the cadets from the stadium.

Events like these were not uncommon during the century- old rivalry between the Longhorns of Austin and the Aggies of College Station. The Longhorn mascot, Bevo, had acquired his name years earlier when the score of 13-0 was branded on his side by some A&M cadets, signifying the score of an Aggie football victory. Prior to the next game, several students from t.u. connected the 13 to make it look like the letter "B." The dash was then altered to look like an "E." A "V" was placed between the E and the zero, hence the name, "BEVO."

The first semester of my eventful senior year came to a close, and I returned to Arkansas for the last of four Christmas breaks. My parents and family knew, by now, that I was a die-hard Aggie through and through. They awaited me with the latest and greatest Aggie joke as I pulled into the driveway. With a brother, Gary, and a sister, Cristy, attending the University of Arkansas, the topic of discussion rarely strayed from one of the two schools during the entire break. Susan, my younger sister, often became the mediator of the debates. After a few weeks of Arkansas snow, I was ready to return to the mild winter climate of College Station.

Basketball season had already begun, and I was anxious to lead yells from within G. Rollie White Coliseum. I enjoyed the basketball games tremendously. We were much closer to the crowd, and it felt much more personal.

One evening during the season we were scheduled to play the Arkansas Razorbacks in G. Rollie White Coliseum and, due to a women's basketball game, the men's game was delayed. Because of the lull, we passed out the campus newspaper for the fans to read while waiting for the varsity game to start. One thing led to another and, by the time the Razorback's starting line up was announced, everyone in the stands acted as if they were reading the paper, ignoring it all.

The Arkansas head coach laughed as he looked into the stands, wondering what was about to happen. Suddenly, they announced the starting line up for A&M and the place went wild! Papers flew everywhere as the Aggies ran on the court. Each subsequent home basketball game, a similar reenactment occurred.

We flew to Louisiana and Arkansas that year in support of the basketball team and, to my knowledge, were the only Aggies in attendance. Being close to the stands at away games had its definite disadvantage. We often found ourselves the brunt of jokes and sarcastic remarks from spectators, some within throwing distance. We somehow managed to ignore it all and kept our sense of humor, though we were often pelted with ice.

During baseball season, we kept somewhat of a lower profile, only performing yells between innings. Most of our time during the baseball season was spent harassing the junior yell leaders, knowing our time at A&M would soon be over. During these games, we often took advantage of the coins taped to the inside of the junior yell leader's traditions book and always had money for a soda or hot dog. We also enjoyed attending the women's softball games and performed yells there, too. Often, the girls on the bench would join in with us as we led yells to those in attendance. After watching the speed at which the women pitched, I was glad to be on the other side of the fence.

Spring arrived and brought with it the annual benefit football game that pitted the Air Force and Aggie Band against the Army, Navy and Marines. Our three-year wait for Elephant Bowl was finally here! We were determined to reverse the Air Force's losing streak.

Practice consisted of two weeks without pads and two weeks of full contact. I soon realized how much it hurt to get hit by a 200 pound college senior and returned to my dorm several evenings slightly incoherent from the collisions.

As the current yell leaders, we were tasked with teaching several freshman the moves to each yell. They had been randomly selected to be the "official" yell leaders for the game. We had an enjoyable time working with them and shared their enthusiasm as they practiced for their big debut in Kyle Field. It reminded me of the time, as a freshman, I had been randomly selected as an Officer of the Day for the Elephant Bowl three years earlier. It meant a great deal to me at the time, and I wanted this to be a fun experience for these freshmen also.

Probst, Roosma, Smiley, Garrett, Yates and I had all decided to play and were determined to create an upset. Game day arrived after a night of thunder and rain. The clouds finally parted, and the sun appeared just prior to kick-off. It caused a humid mist to rise from the artificial turf as the moisture from the wet field evaporated.

We took the field first on defense with Smiley at safety, Roosma at defensive end, and Yates and I as linebackers. After only three plays, I was already winded. The wet field, coupled with the humidity, eventually soaked into my uniform and added what felt like several extra pounds of weight. Knowing we were not in the best of condition, our coach had brought oxygen for us to use while on the sidelines, which I took advantage of with regularity. Yates and I were constantly directed to blitz from our linebacking positions in an attempt to keep the Marine offensive line off guard. Roosma joined us from his defensive end position, crisscrossing to capitalize on any weakness we could find. My feet became so heavy from the moisture, I eventually had to remove a pair of socks, hoping it would help lighten the load.

The game became a defensive battle and remained scoreless throughout the first half. Finally, we scored on a long drive in the fourth quarter and led seven to zero. We were ecstatic.

"Way to go, Garrett," I yelled as he ran off the field from his line position. "All we've gotta do now is hold 'em!"

Time was quickly running out. On our next offensive possession we were unable to move the ball, so I was sent in to punt from deep within our own end zone. As I received the snap, I took two steps forward and kicked the ball. Suddenly, I heard a "thud" and watched the ball bounce backwards through our own goal post. Everyone stood there and looked at each other, wondering what had just happened.

It seems one of my teammates had backed up to assist in a block, and unknowingly, had stepped in my path. The ball ricocheted off of his helmet and bounced backwards through our own goal post.

"Way to go Quinn!" the coach yelled from the sidelines. "You just kicked a field goal for the other team!

I turned, disappointedly, and watched as two points were added to the Marine score.

"Maybe if I don't say anything," I thought to myself, "everyone will think the punt was blocked by one of the rushers on the other team."

Amidst the confusion, we were forced to punt from our own 20-yard line. We eventually held on to win the game by the score of seven to two. We were elated and celebrated like there was no tomorrow. Victory was ours and we were ecstatic. We had redeemed the Air Force once again!

"That ought to hold 'em for a couple of years," Yates said as we all posed for a picture.

"It'll hold me for a lifetime," I responded as our hands met high above our heads.

After an extra long steam shower, we met at Sparkey's to celebrate our long awaited victory. We recounted the perfect blocks and tackles made that day over and over again. Of course, each story grew in exaggeration as the evening progressed. Roosma had imagined at least a dozen quarterback sacks that no one else remembered seeing. Probst recounted three touchdown runs that for some reason were never recorded on the score board. Garret claimed to have been responsible for the perfect block that allowed for our only score of the game. I attempted to change the subject each time the story of my self-inflicted, blocked punt was mentioned.

My neck was sore from a hit I had made on an opposing player while returning one of my other punts. The receiver had made it past everyone and I hit him head-on. It was one of those tackles that defensive players lay awake at night dreaming about. We collided near the sidelines and both of us went crashing into the players standing near the benches. As I got up and walked back onto the field, I felt a thud on the back of my helmet. He had apparently thrown the ball at me out of frustration. I just looked back and smiled, knowing we had the victory in the bag.

After basking in our upset for several days, and ribbing as many Army and Navy cadets as possible, life pretty much returned to normal. The Military Ball was fast approaching, which seemed to indicate our time at Texas A&M was nearing its end. We rented black bow ties and cummerbunds to match our formal cadet uniform and attempted to acquire dates for the event.

Military Ball always seemed to be something right out of a 1940's black and white war movie. Members of the Aggie Band played ball-

room dance music while we tried to pretend we all knew how to properly dance. Most of us did the two- step, or one of the other steps we had
learned at the various dance halls in the area.

"What happened to all that money your parents gave you, Quinn?"
Roy Brantly, the commander of the Ross Volunteers, asked during the
evening as we danced with our dates.

"What money?" I questioned.

"The money your mother gave you for dancing lessons!"

"Hey, you ain't no Fred Astaire yourself!" I hollered back. After the
dance we strolled the campus, chatting about our experiences of the last
four years. We knew Final Review was only a couple of weeks away, and
it would be here before we knew it.

"I can't believe we're going to be former students in a few weeks,"
Roosma remarked as we passed the fish pond.

His words seemed to elicit a strange feeling within me. Part of me was
ready to graduate, yet another part of me wanted to stay somehow. It
was a strange feeling. I knew I couldn't turn back the hands of time,
but I simply wanted to delay the end of my senior year as long as possible. It had taken us so long to get where we were, and the thought of it
ending hadn't really crossed my mind until now. I suppose it was just
that I had come to appreciate Texas A&M more with each passing year.
I loved the friendly atmosphere, the people, and the common bond of
being an Aggie, and knew I would miss it tremendously after graduation.

The Corps at A&M had taught me several things, the most important
being that the amount of respect a person receives is based entirely upon
what he or she achieves as a team player, not upon name or money. I
suddenly realized that real friends can be counted on, no matter what.
Religious beliefs, ethnic origin, and social status have nothing to do with
being an Aggie. I certainly knew I could not buy respect at A&M, as I
always ran low on funds at the end of each semester.

I had always tried to plan inexpensive dates during my senior year.
One particular evening I went dancing with Susie Wall, a young lady I
had met in my Economics class. I chose The Texas Hall of Fame dance
hall on a Wednesday night for our first date, knowing it was student
night and there would be no cover charge. I don't know whether or not
Susie knew I was broke, but she only drank water the entire evening.

As Probst and I stayed out late chatting about our time at Texas A&M, we agreed there was something special about the bond of being an Aggie. Something intangible, impossible to explain. We somehow knew that even though we were about to graduate and go our separate ways, we would return time and time again, regardless of the distance. We knew we would someday join with old friends and classmates, to reminisce about our years at Aggieland and rekindle the spirit within that had united us as cadets. I began to understand why Texas A&M had one of the strongest and most supportive Former Student Associations in the nation.

"Former students. Sounds funny, doesn't it?" I said as we strolled back to the quad after dropping off our dates.

"Who would have ever thought it would happen four years ago," Probst said with a smile.

"Guess we'd better start planning our 15-year class reunion," I said as we entered the dorm. "Want to make a wager on who will have the most kids?"

"You're on!" he replied as we shook hands and entered the dorm.

CHAPTER 18

FORMER STUDENTS

wakened by the persistent buzz of my alarm, I slowly rose from my bed. As I placed my feet on the floor, a gleam of light reflecting off of my senior boots caught my eye. A group of us had stayed up late polishing our boots for the last time so they would look good for the final trip around the drill field. I gazed at them for a moment, visualizing the cadet who was probably dreaming about wearing them later that day. I had decided to sell the boots for one hundred dollars, knowing new senior boots were costing more than $400, and there were many who could not afford them. I had purchased mine used the previous year from another cadet for the same price.

Probst rolled off the top bunk and together we staggered out into the hall to shower. We were surprised to see several juniors standing around in their freshly shined senior boots. "Get 'em off!" Probst grumbled. "We ain't dead yet!"

"Oh, yes you are," Hood, a stubborn junior, yelled back. "Today's Final Review, now roll on over and die like a couple of good old elephants."

"Let 'em be," I whispered to Probst. "He's right. We're dead. It's their outfit now."

"I know. I just don't want them to know it yet."

His words caused me to chuckle as I remembered how anxious we were to assume control of the outfit only a year earlier. I could easily sense their excitement and knew they could hardly wait for the second pass when they would wear their boots in public for the first time.

From the crack in the shower window I could see the all too familiar sight of families gathering on the quad in anticipation of Final Review. Parents beamed with pride as their sons and daughters exited the dorms to meet them. I'm sure many of them never imagined they would see the day when their son or daughter marched in Final Review. Each of these cadets had probably returned home sometime during their freshman year with thoughts of quitting, only to be encouraged to stick it out.

I returned to my room and put on the senior uniform for the last time. It was a relief to know this would be the final time I would have to wear those annoying boot straps around my waist, yet deep down I had somehow loved every minute of it. I strapped on the symbolic spurs, perfected my tuck and roll one last time, and stepped from the room.

"Well, old lady," Probst said as we walked down the stairs. "I guess this is it."

"Yea, it's been fun," I said. "and I wouldn't have traded a minute of it for the world."

"Me neither," he replied as he placed his arm around me. We exited the dorm for the last time as zips and walked with the rest of the seniors toward the outfit.

The spirit was jovial as we formed on the drill field for the last time as members of the Aggie Corps of Cadets. We shook hands with every Gator and expressed appreciation, wishing each cadet luck in the future.

The roles had now strangely reversed. I could sense the anticipation behind me as we formed up on the front row. The juniors could hardly contain their emotion as they jokingly reminded us of who controlled the outfit now.

I remembered my first Final Review as a fish, when I had performed the maneuvers with the guide-on. Time had literally flown by. The last four years now seemed like a blur. I tried to soak it all in as I stood there, knowing in a few short minutes it would all be over. Each of us would take a different path, not knowing if we would all ever be able to get together again.

"All right, Gators, form up!" Smiley shouted for the last time. A loud "Whoop!" was let out by the entire junior class.

"Knock it off," Neese replied. "We ain't officially dead till we're off the drill field."

That all too familiar tingle shot up my spine as the Aggie Band struck the first few notes of the *Aggie War Hymn*. The spirit swelled within me as we prepared to step off.

"Let's go out in style, Zips!" Yates hollered over the noise as we were given the command.

"Bingo, baby!" Ogdee hollered. It echoed back from the crowd causing all of the seniors to "whoop!"

The reviewing stand was in clear view as we made our final left hand turn. Several military officers from all branches of the service were standing in preparation for review of the troops. Surrounding them were hundreds of guests and visitors. I spotted my mom and dad next to the reviewing stand. They had driven up from Arkansas earlier in the week. Dad had the movie camera pointed in our direction. Movies had been a part of our family life from the first year of their marriage.

"This is it, Gators," Garrett said as we approached the stand.

"Make it look good!" Roosma yelled.

Suddenly, the command was given.

"Squadron, eyes right!" Smiley shouted as we snapped our heads to a 45-degree angle and simultaneously saluted the officers to our right. As they raised their right hands to return our salute, my mind instantly reeled off a kaleidoscopic sequel of images from the past several years: quaddings, crap outs, midnight yell practices, road trips, bonfires, dances and football games. The visions raced through my mind like a high speed film.

"Was it all just a dream?" I wondered, struggling to hold my salute. "Did all of that really happen? How could I have been so lucky to have been able to experience it all?"

I visualized the faces of friends I had made. I knew I would miss them while in Europe. I had just accepted an assignment with the Air Force in Germany. I wondered what the coming years would bring and how each of our lives would change. My illusions were shattered by Smiley's final command, "Squadron, ready front!"

We dropped our salute and snapped our heads to the front. Reality set in. It was over. Each senior instinctively reached to grasp the other. Arm in arm, we led the outfit to the end of the drill field. My emotions suddenly took control, and tears began to blur my vision as we continued to march. Through the blur I could make out others around me crying also.

We crossed the street, allowing the other units to exit the field, and gathered on the sidewalk. Amidst tears and hugs, final farewells were given to the other cadets in the outfit as rain began to fall. I had never seen or experienced such an outpouring of emotion before and was unaccustomed to it. Smiley gathered the outfit together for one final outfit yell as the rain turned into a downpour.

"One, two, three," we began in unison. "Fighting Gator Two! The best! The boldest! The best damn outfit anywhere!"

I now truly felt what I had only dreamed of that night after midnight yell practice my freshman year. I watched as our fish continued to wild-cat, arms raised high, as if in tribute to us. I finally understood what it meant to be an Aggie. All of the sweat and agony of the past several years was now worth every second, if only for this one brief moment in time.

One by one, each member of Squadron Two approached to express their appreciation and to say good-bye, ignoring the storm that had broken out. I realized then that what probably meant the most was the fact that there was a slight chance that I, along with the rest of my class, may have influenced someone's life for the better. The Corps of Cadets at Texas A&M, I surmised, had not only changed me, but had dramatically improved an insurmountable number of lives over the past hundred years, for the better. What had we learned? Honor, devotion, commitment to name a few of the traits. Things not easily learned in a short period of time.

An hour later the clouds parted allowing the sun to shine through just as the new Corps formed at the opposite side of the drill field. It was a fitting tribute, seemingly to signify the beginning of a new chapter in the history of the Corps. The juniors beamed with pride as they strolled by wearing their senior boots for the first time.

"Looking sharp, zips!" McAnally shouted as they formed up. The sophomores seemed to walk with increased confidence, now wearing their white belts which symbolized their official promotion to Surgebutts. Then came the freshmen, smiling with ecstasy, knowing they had made it past the hard part. All they lacked now was a new freshman class to whip into shape.

"Go get 'em, Gators!" Garrett yelled as they stepped off as a brand new outfit.

We let out a loud "WHOOP!" as they passed in front of the reviewing stand. It was strange to watch them march without us. It had been four years since I had watched the Corps from outside of its ranks.

"What a difference a few years can make," I told Jumper as we turned to leave. A look of blankness seemed to transport him into the past.

"Yea, it won't be long, and we'll be back here to watch our kids march in final review," he finally said causing me to laugh and lose my breath. ...

"Come on, dad! I know you can do at least one more push up!" Martin yelled as his little brother Ryan bounced on my back. "If I can do ten push ups all by myself, does that mean I can be a Texas Aggie when I grow up?"

I looked at him and smiled.

"You bet, fish Quinn," I said as he and Ryan smiled. "I have a feeling you two are going to tear 'em up."

GLOSSARY

Aggie: a student at Texas A&M University or a former student of the same.

Aggieland: Texas A&M University, College Station, Texas

Aggie Muster: An annual tribute held throughout the world paid to deceased Aggies.

Ascot: A piece of cloth worn with the Aggie Corps uniform during special occasions.

B.Q.: Literally, "band queer". A nickname for Aggie band members.

Bad bull: A joke taken too far or something bad.

Bag Monster: An imaginary monster that makes cadets oversleep.

Bevo: The University of Texas (t.u.) mascot.

Bider: The hat worn by cadets.

Black belt: Nickname for a freshman or sophomore.

Boot straps: Elastic chords worn around the waist to hold a cadet's shirt down tight.

Bonfire: Timber set ablaze prior to the annual football game with t.u.

Brass: Insignia worn on the Aggie uniform.

Bust butt: To run.

C.O.: The commanding officer; the senior in charge of a unit.

C.Q.: Call to Quarters; the period cadets should be studying.

C.T.: A nickname given to cadets not in the Aggie Band. Literally, it stands for "Corps Turds".

Campusology: Historical questions about Texas A&M University that each cadet is required to learn during his freshman year.

Chow: Meals.

Class set: The number of push-ups that equal the class graduation year, ie: 81 push-ups would equal a class set for a member of the class of 1981.

Corps: Short for the Corps of Cadets.

Corps staff: Cadets in charge of the Corps of Cadets.

Crap out: Exercise, normally for discipline reasons.

Crapper: The restroom.

Double time: To run while in formation.

Douche out: The act of throwing water on a sleeping upperclassman, normally performed by freshmen.

Drop handle: The authorization for a fish to call an upperclassman by his or her first name.

Drop: Assume the position for push-ups.

Duncan: The name of the cadet dining hall.

Elephant: A senior at Texas A&M

Elephant Bowl: An annual football game between Corps seniors.

Elephant Walk: The senior class's final stroll through campus.

Eyes right: A command used to salute while marching.

F.O.W.: The first week of training for new freshman in the Corps. Literally, Fish Orientation Week.

Fart off: An insult made about another cadet's unit.

First sergeant: The junior in charge of an outfit.

Final review: The last march for seniors and the formal exchange of leadership within the Corps.

Fish: Freshman at Texas A&M University.

Fish buddy: What fish call each other.

Fish Camp: An orientation camp for all incoming freshmen.

Fish Drill Team: A freshman military drill team chosen to compete in military drill competitions.

Fish bite: A very small bite of food taken by fish while eating.

Fish Jones: A generic term for any fish unknown to upperclassmen.

Fish spurs: Bottle caps worn on the shoes prior to the SMU football game.

Frog: A cadet that enrolls in the Corps of Cadets after the start of school.

Football: What Aggies eat, sleep, drink and breath.

G. Rollie White: The coliseum on campus.

Gator: A member of Squadron Two.

Ghost: A member of the Ross Volunteers when wearing a white uniform.

Gig: A bad mark against a cadet.

Good bull: Something good, positive or humorous.

Guide on: An outfit flag.

Hole: A fish's room.

Humping it: The act of bending over to yell.

Jody: A rhythmic song or poem performed while marching.

Kyle Field: The football stadium on campus.

March-in: Drill competition between outfits, normally prior to football games.

March to the Brazos: Annual Corps benefit march for the March of Dimes.

Military Ball: An annual dance held for the Corps of Cadets.

M.S.C.: The Memorial Student Center, the student building on campus.

Non Reg: Student at Texas A&M not enrolled in the Corps of Cadets.

O.D.: Officer of the Day. Senior in charge for the day or seniors assigned to guard the football field during football games.

Old lady: A nickname for roommate.

Parson's Mounted Cavalry: Cadets assigned to a special unit that rides horseback.

Pisshead: A sophomore.

Pull out: Assuming a privilege not yet earned.

Quad: The location on campus where the Corps is located.

Quadding: The act of dropping water from a dorm room, on a cadet, from at least one story high.

Red pot: Cadets in charge of building the bonfire each year.

Ram: An extremely bad mark against a cadet.

Reveille: The official mascot of Texas A&M University, a collie, and the highest ranking cadet on campus.

Ross Volunteer: A member of the National Honor Guard for the Governor of Texas. Members are selected among juniors and seniors within the Corps.

Steam shower: A hot shower normally reserved for juniors and seniors.

Stick: A specially cut board designed to lock a cadet in his room from the outside.

Surgebutt: A cadet junior.

Senior boots: Riding boots worn only by seniors in the Corps.

Silver Taps: A tribute to deceased Aggies held on campus each month.

T-sip: A student at t.u.

Twelfth Man: The name for the student body of Texas A&M University.

Whip out: Unique form of introduction used by freshmen when introducing themselves to upperclassmen.

White belt: A junior or senior in the Corps.

Wild catting: Expression of exhilaration.

Whoop!: A term used only by juniors or seniors to express joy.

Yell practice: A gathering of Aggie Students practicing school yells. It is normally held at midnight prior to a football game.

Zip: A senior.

W H E R E   T H E Y   A R E   N O W
(From the Front Cover)

1. John Neese served in the Air Force as a Missile Control Officer and is now employed by Applied Materials as an operations planner. He lives in Plano.

2. Brian Yates is now a consultant for Southwest Environmental and a professional body builder. He now lives in Ventura, California.

3. Tim Garrett is a sales representative for Glazer's Wholesale in Dallas where he resides with his wife, Cheryl.

4. Tom Jumper, after serving as a C-141 pilot in the Air Force, flies for American Airlines. He now lives in Dallas with his wife, Lynn.

5. Mike Ogdee is a financial examiner in Houston where he audits several financial institutions.

6. Jason Roosma, after serving with the Air Force as a C-141 pilot, flies for Delta Airlines. He is also a training consultant for Hughes Aircraft. He lives in Bedford, Texas, with his wife, Cindy, and their two daughters and one son.

7. Dan Quinn served as air weapons control officer in the Air Force and is now a mission coordinator for an air-to-air combat range at Hill AFB in Utah. He resides in Roy, Utah with his wife, Cindy, and their two sons and one daughter. Their fourth child is due in May of 1993.

8. Mike Probst is managing editor of the Rock Port Pilot newspaper where he resides with his wife, Diane, and their three daughters.

9. Mike Smiley is an attorney and practices law in Amarillo. He resides there with his wife, Jana, and their son.

10. Mark McAnally is an independent real estate appraiser. He and his wife, Teresa, live in San Antonio.